Table of Contents

The Incarnate and the Impoverished

Bridging Theology and Social Advocacy

by

Dr. ant

The Incarnate and the Impoverished: Bridging Theology and Social Advocacy

Contents

Introduction

The pastiche of Catholic doctrine is richly adorned with fibril that span across centuries, capturing both the profound and the practical dimensions of human existence. In this interwoven narrative, two distinct strands emerge: the commitment to social justice and the defense of faith through apologetics. While they may seem disparate at first glance, a closer examination reveals a deep-seated connection between them, especially when it comes to the tenet of the "Option for the Poor and Vulnerable" and the theological justification of the divinity of Jesus Christ.

Our exploration begins with an understanding of Catholic Social Justice as a profound commitment that transcends mere charity. It represents a structured and theologically rooted imperative to stand with the marginalized and to advocate for systemic changes that reflect the inherent dignity of every person. This principle is not just a call to assist the needy but a reminder of the moral duty to transform unjust structures. The "Option for the Poor" thus challenges us to identify and rectify societal inequities with an urgency that reflects the teachings of Christ himself.

Parallel to this social ethos lies the rigorous discipline of apologetics, tasked with defending the tenets of faith amidst the skepticism woven into modern discourse. Christian apologetics, especially concerning the divinity of Jesus, engages with reason and belief, inviting dialogue with both adherents and critics. It is a journey through historical, scriptural, and doctrinal landscapes, unearthing evidence to illuminate and affirm the identity of Christ as more than a historical figure—as a divine one.

In this intellectual odyssey, we come to recognize the harmonious resonance between advocating for the marginalized and proclaiming the divine nature of Jesus. The Gospels continually underscore Jesus' profound identification with the poor, a reflection of both his human empathy and divine mission. His life invites us to consider how true divinity is shown not through dominance, but through service, especially to those on the periphery of society.

The tension between faith and reason is neither new nor resolvable in simple terms. Yet, the cross-pollination between social justice and apologetics presents a compelling narrative for the modern world, particularly within Catholic thought. Their intersection beckons theologians, sociologists, and believers alike to explore doctrines that are often viewed in isolation.

An intricate dance exists between the call to action towards justice and the rational defense of divine mysteries. This does not imply a compromise but rather a synthesis, where each element enriches the other. The commitment to social justice becomes not only an ethical mandate but a testament to the truth of Christ's teachings. Correspondingly, the apologetic defense of Jesus as the Son of God finds its most poignant expression in the lived reality of service to the least among us.

Furthermore, the theological reflections embedded in social justice and apologetics invite an allegorical interpretation. Jesus, as depicted in the Gospels, often speaks in parables—a method that transcends direct didactic teaching and invites deeper contemplation. These stories, rich with layers of meaning, challenge both the believer and the thinker to delve beyond the surface, questioning, interpreting, and ultimately integrating these lessons into life's moral and spiritual fabric.

In embracing a philosophically and historically informed perspective, we appreciate the crucial role of the Church Fathers in shaping an understanding of how faith and action are intertwined. Their writings offer a treasure trove of insight, blending the divine and the ethical in ways that continue to resonate today. They remind us that our journey isn't just one of personal salvation but one interwoven with communal responsibility.

As we navigate through this book, the goal is to unearth the foundations and implications of these two cornerstones of Catholic doctrine. By reconciling and paralleling these pathways—social justice and apologetics—we aspire to reflect a cohesiveness that is as intellectually satisfying as it is spiritually enriching. This reflective space serves not as a conclusion but as a perpetual call to action and belief, a reminder that stillness is contrary to both faith and justice.

Chapter 1: Foundations of Catholic Social Justice

The foundations of Catholic social justice form a mosaic assembled from enduring principles that have echoed through millennia, inviting a vivid reflection on the collective hope for a just society. At its heart, this chapter reflects upon the vibrant intersection where theology meets the call for action, exploring doctrines that challenge the faithful to embrace the marginalized with fervor and compassion. Within the rich traditions of the Church, the voice of Catholic social teaching emerges as both echo and prophecy, rooted deeply in a faith that dares to look poverty in the eye and respond with love and care. The principle of the Option for the Poor and Vulnerable stands as a testament to this call, intertwining the fate of the least with the boundless mystery of divine incarnation. In this interplay of love and struggle, truth and grace, one glimpses a profound narrative—it's more than ethics or charity, it's the very reflection of a Christ who walked among us, embodying hope and justice. This chapter embarks on a journey through this narrative, seeking not just to inform but to inspire a living commitment that aligns the soul's yearning for the divine with the duty to elevate the dignity of all.

Overview of Catholic Social Teaching

In the luminous agglomeration of Catholic social teaching, a profound vision of justice and love emerges, guiding the faithful toward a world where human dignity and the common good stand unassailable. At its core lies an intricate interplay of moral principles that echo through history with a resonant clarity, insisting on a preferential option for the poor and vulnerable. This isn't merely an abstract notion but a call to action, grounded in the empathetic embrace of humanity's weaknesses and potentialities. With both poetic grace and sharp allegorical wit, these teachings unfurl as a philosophical compass, pointing towards the divine model personified in Jesus Christ. They do not whisper of charity alone but herald a wider transformation—a dynamic harmony between justice and apologetics, wherein the defence of Christ's divinity and the upliftment of the downtrodden coalesce into a singular evangelical call that transcends systems, inviting endless reflection and renewed commitment from theologians and laity alike.

Historical Context of Social Justice unveils a system developed over centuries, constituent elements of which are essential to understanding Catholic Social Justice.

In the annals of history, social justice didn't begin as a defined concept. It emerged from the crucible of human civilization, parallel to the development of social systems and religious thought. Its roots can be traced back to antiquity, where human societies grappled with the inequalities intrinsic to settled life and economies. In this context, justice was a matter for philosophers and theologians, who both pondered its nature and championed its practice. The early Christian community, with its radical calls for mutual aid and shared resources, demonstrates an innate alignment with social justice principles long before they were named as such.

The Hebrew Scriptures provided early examples with their insistence on protecting widows, orphans, and foreigners. Such Old Testament injunctions foresaw a world where charity was more than an individual good. Rather, it became a structural necessity grounded in divine command. The New Testament amplified this with Christ's radical exhortations in the Gospels—"Blessed are the poor," "Love your neighbor," and the imperative for care exemplified in the parable of the Good Samaritan. These teachings weren't just spiritual guidelines; they were blueprints for a communal ethic of justice.

As we traverse history into the Middle Ages, figures like Thomas Aquinas synthesized Aristotelian philosophy and Christian thought, carving a place for justice within Catholic doctrine. Aquinas's work pointed beyond legalistic interpretations of justice towards encompassing notions that included mercy and charity. His writing laid the groundwork for understanding justice as inherently social, echoing Divine order while promoting human dignity. Moreover, the Church, with its canon laws and councils, gradually wove this understanding into the fabric of its social doctrine.

By the time of the Industrial Revolution, humanity faced a seismic shift—a shift marked by burgeoning capitalism and unparalleled human suffering. The Catholic Church, often slow to respond, eventually found its voice through papal encyclicals that addressed the urgent need for social justice. "Rerum Novarum" in 1891 marked a turning point, where Pope Leo XIII articulated the necessity for ethical considerations in economic life, the rights of laborers, and the moral responsibility of wealth.

We find this dynamic continue through the 20th century, as theologians, philosophers, and papal voices harmonized to form what is known today as Catholic Social Teaching. The work of articulating social justice became not just a theoretical exercise, but an urgent imperative, deeply entwined with the Church's mission. The Second Vatican Council (1962-1965) breathed new life into these discussions, emphasizing the Church's responsibility to advocate for justice in both local and global contexts. The Council's documents underscored the notion that genuine faith must evidence itself through action in the world.

Catholic Social Teaching, thus, coalesced into a guiding framework, neatly capturing a lineage of theological reflection and active concern. The principle of the Option for the Poor and Vulnerable emerged as a key element within this teaching, emphasizing that societies should be judged by how they treat their most marginalized members. It's in this context where apologetics for the divinity of Jesus Christ and social justice meet, with the figure of Christ serving as the divine exemplar for self-giving love and justice.

In conclusion, the historical context of social justice within Catholicism is a narrative of evolution and continuity—a testament to a tradition that has sought over millennia to translate divine love into human action. It challenges us to perceive justice not merely as an abstract ideal but as a lived reality shaped by faith. As we carry forth this legacy, the imperative remains: to let our actions speak for our beliefs, aligning earthly justice with heavenly mandate.

The Principle of Option for the Poor and Vulnerable

In the complex house of cards of Catholic social justice, the Principle of Option for the Poor and Vulnerable emerges as both a moral compass and a vivid echo of Christ's incarnational mystery. This principle charges the faithful to champion the cause of the marginalized, not merely as an act of charity but as an intrinsic reflection of divine love. As the poor and vulnerable occupy a sacred space reminiscent of Christ's humble earthly journey, they invite us to a deeper solidarity that transcends mere social obligation and touches on the very essence of Christology. When we consider this option, we're propelled into the dynamic interplay between justice and divine empathy; it's here that apologetic discourse intertwines with social action, as our defense of Christ's divinity aptly mirrors our defense of human dignity. Thus, in opting for the poor, we affirm a theological narrative where vulnerability is both a spiritual and societal crucible, unlocking profound insights into the incarnation and the living Gospel. This choice transforms the believer, knitting temporal acts of justice with the eternal truth of Christ's love.

Biblical Foundations The Principle of Option for the Poor and Vulnerable is deeply rooted in the Biblical narrative, and it's imperative to explore this connection to fully comprehend its pivotal role within Catholic social justice. The Scriptures are not merely a collection of ancient texts but a living testament, vibrant with themes of justice, mercy, and a preferential option for the marginalized. The Bible, in its rich tapestry, weaves an enduring message: the care for the poor and vulnerable is intrinsic to the practice of true faith.

Throughout the Old Testament, there is a constant exhortation to remember the widow, the orphan, and the stranger. These are not mere injunctions; they are fundamental to the covenantal relationship between God and His people. From the laws of Leviticus to the poetic yearnings of the Psalms, the poor are not forgotten but are called to the forefront as a measure of society's righteousness. The Jubilee Year, a radical vision of economic reset, underscores this principle, reminding us of a God who desires equity among His creation. This divine decree challenges systemic injustices, portraying a cosmic justice where human dignity is placed above material wealth.

The prophets echo this divine mandate with fervent voices. Isaiah, Jeremiah, and Amos, among others, rise against nations and leaders who neglect the poor. Their words serve as a clarion call against complacency and a reminder of divine retribution against those who foster inequality. They assert plainly that neglect of the poor is tantamount to abandoning God Himself. Amos' cry for justice to "roll down like waters" is not a passive wish but an urgent appeal for action, one that transcends time and resonates today.

In the New Testament, Jesus Himself embodies this option for the poor and vulnerable. His inaugural sermon in Luke presents Him reading from Isaiah, declaring a mission to bring good news to the poor and freedom to the oppressed, weaving a continuity between the ancient prophecies and His work. His ministry mirrors these convictions not through grandiose acts but through simple, profound gestures of love: feeding the hungry, healing the sick, and welcoming the outcast. These are not merely miracles but acts of divine justice, affirmations of God's preference for the vulnerable. Jesus, in His radical love, raises the destitute to the forefront of His kingdom's manifesto.

The Beatitudes, a cornerstone of Christ's teachings, articulate the values of his Kingdom with striking clarity. "Blessed are the poor in spirit," He proclaims, a paradox that upends societal norms and redefines power dynamics. These blessings, far from being merely poetic, are a seismic shift in understanding divine favor and human constructs of worth. In aligning Himself with the marginalized, Jesus does not just offer solidarity but a transformative vision where the last are made first.

It is paramount to recognize how Jesus' parables consistently illustrate the divine option for society's least and last. The parables of the Good Samaritan and the Rich Man and Lazarus demand a reevaluation of neighborliness and a rejection of indifference. They strip away superficial legalism, revealing a heart responsive to the plight of others as the true essence of the Law. Through such stories, Christ invites his followers into a radical kinship with the poor, establishing a community bound by compassion.

Furthermore, the Acts of the Apostles and early Christian communities embodied this biblical framework, living out the Gospel's radical hospitality and shared resources. The communal life of believers was not simply a social experiment but a lived theology, where the option for the poor was actualized, and possessions were seen as communal, dissolving barriers between giver and receiver.

The Apostle Paul's writings, while doctrinal, bolster this commitment. His collection for the Jerusalem Church serves as a testament to the unity and solidarity across cultural and economic divides. It is a tangible expression of the ecclesial body's inseparable bond with its weakest members. Paul's epistles consistently call the faithful to embody agape love, steadfast in service to others, echoing Christ's incarnational approach.

In examining these biblical foundations, the integration and indistinguishability of faith and justice become clear. Catholic Social Teaching, particularly through the principle of option for the poor, is not an innovation but a continuation of this biblical heritage. It is a reaffirmation that justice is election of love for those who are marginalized. The Church's recognition of this calls for a reenactment of these sacred stories in our contemporary world, a living testimony turning scripture to reality.

Ultimately, exploring these biblical foundations urges us, as followers of Christ, to see through the lenses of divine love and justice. It implores an integrated spiritual and social vision, where our advocacy is not symbolic but substantive, mirroring the life of Jesus who aligned Himself with the powerless. In understanding this divine option, we encounter not only a call for societal transformation but the profound revelation of God's Kingdom, already among us and yet to come.

For scholars and theologians, this exploration lays fertile ground for dialogue between Scripture and social action, compelling us to discern and implement the transcendent truth that beckons toward a Gospel-driven justice. To engage in this endeavor is to find ourselves caught up in the sacred drama, transforming sacred narrative into living reality, and writing our lives into the enduring story of a just and compassionate God.

Chapter 2: Understanding Apologetics

In the ever-evolving dialogue between faith and reason, apologetics emerges as an intellectual amalgam construed with the fibers of conviction and inquiry. It's both an art and a science, striving to articulate the coherence of divine mysteries, particularly the divinity of Jesus Christ, within the realms of human understanding. By tracing its historical roots, one finds apologetics intricately linked to the Church Fathers, whose voices resonate through time, crafting persuasive arguments and offering a robust defense of the faith. This chapter embarks on an exploration of these defenses, demonstrating how they not only affirm the divinity of Christ but also reflect the Catholic ethos of an option for the poor and vulnerable. Here, apologetics isn't merely about defending doctrines but about revealing the deep-seated compassion at Christianity's heart, where reason and love converge to illuminate the path toward a just society. Through this lens, the rich heritage of apologetic tradition offers not just answers, but a call to an active, loving participation in the divine narrative.

Definition and Purpose of Apologetics

Apologetics serves both as a defense and as a beacon, illuminating the core truths of the Christian faith, particularly the divinity of Jesus Christ. It's not merely an intellectual exercise but a purposeful endeavor to bridge faith and reason, nurturing a dialogue between belief and skepticism. This discipline aims to articulate faith's rationale to seekers and skeptics alike, grounding its assertions with historical, philosophical, and theological scaffolding. The essence of apologetics, much like the Catholic Social Justice tenet of the Option for the Poor and Vulnerable, lies in its commitment to truth and compassion, asserting that faith is not an isolated island but a living testimony with tangible implications for human dignity and equity. It's an eloquent dance between heart and intellect, seeking not only to affirm but also to understand, explore, and ultimately share the profound mystery of divine love embodied in Christ. In this sense, apologetics becomes a vessel for both truth and transformation, offering answers that resonate with the complexities of human experience.

Historical Overview In the vast and rich deposit of theology, the weaving of apologetics has endured as a dynamic and multifaceted thread, shimmering with historical vigor and intellectual rigor. Its emergence isn't a mere footnote in Christian thought but a vital chord that has been continuously strummed throughout the epochs of Christian history. The journey of apologetics, from its embryonic beginnings in the early Christian era to the sophisticated discourse of the present day, illustrates the evolution of defending the faith through reason and dialogue, a theme recurrent in Christian intellectual endeavor.

The origin of Christian apologetics can be situated within a society that was often hostile to the nascent sect of followers of Jesus. In the first centuries after Christ, amid the bustling, polytheistic milieu of the Roman Empire, early apologists such as Justin Martyr and Tertullian stood as intellectual shields against accusations hurled at Christianity. Their writings formed a bulwark against misconceptions, offering reasoned defenses of the faith's veracity and addressing the perplexities posed by critics. Unlike modern scribes cloistered from the imminence of persecution, these apologists faced potential martyrdom, adding a visceral urgency to their works.

As Christianity secured legitimacy and took its place at the forefront of Roman society with the Edict of Milan, the nature of apologetics transformed. Questions no longer solely revolved around the truth of Christian claims against pagan critiques but expanded to include theological disputes within Christianity itself. It was in the crucible of such debates that the councils of Nicaea and Chalcedon were forged, birthing creeds that remain central to Christian orthodoxy. Apologetics thus grew to encompass a defence against both external skepticism and internal heresy, delineating the contours of orthodoxy.

In medieval times, apologetics was primarily the domain of theologians and philosophers who saw the harmony between faith and reason as fundamental. Thinkers like Thomas Aquinas encapsulated this ethos, with his magnum opus, "Summa Theologica," presenting an elaborate system of faith buttressed by Aristotelian logic. The scholastic tradition found in Aquinas and Anselm embraced the dance between reason and revelation, weaving a fabric of theodicy, ontology, and divine nature that captivated the intellectual currents of the time.

Yet, as the medieval world yielded to the Renaissance and then to the Reformation, apologetic discourse was reshaped anew. The Reformers, with their clarion call for sola scriptura, inevitably turned apologetics towards scripture's primacy, re-engaging with scriptural texts to illuminate doctrines long obscured by ecclesiastical accretions. Concurrently, the Catholic response materialized as the Counter-Reformation, where the Council of Trent asserted a robust defense of Catholic doctrine. In this tumult, apologetics was not passive but active, engaging adversaries in dialectic over the nature and purview of Christian truths.

With the Enlightenment, a new epoch of revitalized skepticism and rationalism dawned, challenging Christianity's intellectual legitimacy on a broader scale. Apologetic efforts in this era, typified by figures like Blaise Pascal and later John Henry Newman, grappled with the discord between an empirically driven worldview and a faith steeped in mystery and transcendence. Pascal's "Pensées" and Newman's "Apologia Pro Vita Sua" reflect nuanced responses to the lyric of doubt that characterized this age, imbuing their work with a sense of persuasive earnestness.

The 19th and 20th centuries heralded transformations in both the global scene and theological inquiry, engendering new approaches within apologetics. Amidst the philosophical upheavals, existential questions about humanity's place and purpose emerged as focal concerns. Within this context, apologetics adapted, engaging not only with atheism and agnosticism but critiquing the secular narratives that sought to usurp religious themes. This era gave rise to celebrated intellectual defenses such as those by G.K. Chesterton and C.S. Lewis, who poetically and philosophically reconciled Christian tenets with modern sensibilities.

Modern apologetics now stands at the crossroads of interdisciplinary engagement and cultural dialogue. The digital age brings fresh challenges and opportunities to apologize in the ancient sense—to give an account and defense of faith. Today's apologists navigate a pluralistic landscape, where dialogues with science, ethics, and other worldviews are paramount. The burgeoning fields of ecology, technology, and social justice beckon apologetics to an expanded role that acknowledges the complex reality of contemporary existence.

Throughout its storied history, apologetics, while primarily tethered to intellectual contests, casts a wider net by intertwining with the heart's concerns. It has never been confined to sterile doctrinal disputes; it carries the heartbeat of empathetic engagement, a testament to the hope and certainty found in the Christian message. From the apostles' early sermons to today's scholarly debates, apologetics has mattered not only because of what it defends but also because of its call to live out a coherent and compassionate faith.

In weaving the historical overview of apologetics into the contemporary discourse on Catholic Social Justice, particularly the Option for the Poor, one finds the enduring legacy of a faith actively defended and a commitment zealously shared. Apologetics remains a living tradition, reinforcing continuity and stimulating dialogues that navigate both the legacy of Jesus's divinity and the Church's social mission. Thus, this historical thread stitches together the doctrinal and the pragmatic, inviting us to reflect anew on the unyielding harmony between faith, reason, and action.

Key Apologetic Arguments for Jesus' Divinity

In the heart of apologetics lies a profound confluence of history and theology, where key arguments for Jesus' divinity illuminate the spiritual and intellectual journey of believers across the ages. These arguments do not merely rest on dogmatic assertions but engage with a rich philosophical and theological discourse that echoes the wisdom of early Church Fathers and resonates through time. The divinity of Jesus is often elucidated through the profound mystery of the Incarnation, spurred by His unparalleled moral teachings and the transformative power of His resurrection, beckoning both the learned and the lay to a deeper understanding of His divine nature. These arguments serve as beacons for the faithful, guiding them to contemplate the paradoxes of Christ's humanity and divinity, much like a parable that challenges the mind while soothing the soul. Thus, in exploring the apologetic defense of Jesus' divinity, one encounters a symphony of logic and faith, a harmonious dance of reason and revelation that offers a sure foundation upon which the tenets of Catholic faith firmly rest.

Patristic Contributions in the realm of apologetics are akin to an ancient river that has carved out a valley of theological thought, shaping and nourishing the landscape of Christian doctrine. The Church Fathers, those formidable architects of early Christian theology, wielded their intellects as both shield and sword, defending the divinity of Christ against the skepticism and heresies of their time. Their contributions stand as monumental witnesses to the profound mysteries of the Incarnation and the Trinity—a subject that would deeply engage any thoughtful sociologist or theologian alike. Through their writings and teachings, they laid a robust foundation upon which future generations would build their understanding of Christ's dual nature, fully God and fully man.

The tapestry woven by the Patristic Fathers is rich with allegorical threads and philosophical insights. In attempting to expound on the divinity of Jesus, they often drew upon the wellspring of Scripture as well as Hellenistic philosophies, weaving together a defense that was both logically rigorous and theologically profound. Consider the writings of Justin Martyr, passionately interlacing reason and revelation to affirm that Christ, the Logos, existed before all temporal creation. His approach was not merely a defense but a bridge—linking the divine mystery to human understanding. Through allegory and metaphor, Justin posited that just as reason forms the essence of philosophical inquiry, Jesus forms the essence of revealed truth.

Similarly, Irenaeus of Lyons, in his theological masterpiece "Against Heresies," mounted a spirited defense against Gnostic dualism. Here, he rallied the faithful around the truth that Jesus, the Word made flesh, was the ultimate revelation of divine love and truth. Irenaeus argued persuasively that Jesus' divinity could not be a mere illusion or a demiurgical trick but was an essential truth that entered into human history. He underscored the necessity of Jesus' incarnation for human salvation—a theme intricately linked with the Church's option for the poor and vulnerable, as it highlights the profound love and solidarity of God with humanity, particularly its most marginalized members.

The oratory splendor of Athanasius rings throughout the corridors of history, echoing his vehement defense against Arianism. Athanasius insisted that Christ was of the same substance as the Father, engaging in a theological battle that would find its resolution in the Nicene Creed. His contributions went beyond mere defenses; they were affirmations of faith that reinforced the very identity and mission of the Church. By asserting Christ's divine nature so emphatically, Athanasius and his contemporaries laid the groundwork for a Christology that recognized Jesus not as a distant deity but as one eternally engaged with human suffering and redemption.

The intersection of apologetics with the principles of social justice, as illuminated by the Patristic Fathers, invites a reflection on how the divinity of Christ influences the Church's concern for the poor. When Gregory of Nazianzus declared, "That which He has not assumed, He has not healed," he was pointing towards the transformative power of the Incarnation—a divine solidarity that elevates and redeems the human condition. In understanding Jesus' divinity, the Church affirms a preferential option for the poor not just as a social imperative but as a theological reflection of Christ's mission on earth. Such patristic insights ensure that the Church's advocacy for the marginalized is more than philanthropy; it's rooted in the sacramental vision of Christ's engagement with humanity.

Ambrose of Milan blended pastoral duty with theological insight, asserting through his homilies and writings that the care of the poor was intrinsic to Christian duty, mirroring Christ's own divine compassion. His thought offers both a defensive and offensive apologetic: that in upholding the divinity and humanity of Christ, one must also accept the implications of His teachings and actions towards the most vulnerable. In the synthesis of theological belief and social practice, Ambrose illustrates perfectly the unity between divine truths and lived ethics, a unity that today's advocates and theologians strive to emulate.

Moreover, the philosophical musings of Augustine present a deep well of wisdom and introspection, pivotal to understanding apologetics in the light of social justice. Augustine's beliefs on the divine light illuminating the human mind resonate with those who see advocacy as not just social obligation, but as enlightenment. His assertion that "our hearts are restless until they rest in You" simultaneously affirms Christ's divinity and implores believers to act in His name, offering rest and justice to the weary and oppressed. Through Augustine, one discerns the eternal ramifications of divine love manifested in human action.

What emerges from the collective wisdom of the Church Fathers is a holistic apologetic narrative that profoundly influences the Catholic understanding of Jesus' divinity. The ancient battles they fought over Christological doctrines are not mere relics of history; they shape and inform the Church's persistent commitment to justice and love in the contemporary world. Their arguments provide a bedrock—a steady foundation upon which the principle of the option for the poor and vulnerable finds its ultimate rationale and expression.

The Fathers remind us that defending the divinity of Christ is not a theoretical exercise removed from the struggles of human life. Rather, it is a vital and dynamic engagement, one that calls for both scholarly rigor and compassionate action. In their writings, it's clear that to accept Jesus as divine is not only to affirm His place in the heavenly order but also to engage actively in the healing and upliftment of humanity. In this light, the apologetics of the Patristic era seamlessly woven with the strands of social justice reflect an enduring and evolving testament to the Faith, one as relevant today as it was in the nascent days of the Church.

Chapter 3: Theological Perspectives on Poverty

To explore the theological perspectives on poverty is to venture into the profound heart of the Gospel, where Christ himself aligns unflinchingly with the impoverished. In the Gospels, Jesus's resonance with poverty isn't merely a social commentary; it's an affirmation of divine love manifest in human limitation. The Church Fathers, in their early teachings, elucidated this through allegories that depicted the humility and servitude of Christ as a model for the faithful. Their insights carved a theological path that champions social justice, underscoring that addressing poverty isn't just a charitable act but a facet of divine justice itself. This theological stance isn't merely academic but is an incarnate call to action, echoing through the corridors of time, challenging believers to entwine their spirituality with acts of mercy. Poverty becomes not just a condition to alleviate but a lens through which the faithful might perceive the divine mystery of God's presence among the least, challenging every disciple to translate their mendicant faith into profound, transformative love.

Jesus and Poverty in the Gospels

In the tapestry of the Gospels, Jesus' engagement with poverty is not merely an anecdotal thread but rather a profound narrative core, reflecting the divine compassion that transcends human barriers. His teachings present an allegorical play, inviting both the pauper and the prince to the same divine banquet, thereby illustrating the radical kinship inherent in God's kingdom. This is not simply philosophical rhetoric but a call to action, urging believers to recognize Christ's visage in the impoverished—a personification of Matthew's Beatitudes and the Magnificat's revolutionary promise. With vivid strokes, Jesus paints in parables and miracles an image of a countercultural economy where the last are first; thus, His actions and words form an apologetic contour revealing His divine nature by the embrace of community over hierarchy and service over dominance. In this living Gospel, poverty is both a spiritual and material reality—a stage where theological truths about divine justice and mercy unfold in the earthly theatre.

Interpretative Approaches in exploring the figure of Jesus and poverty as presented in the Gospels unveils a Person enlivened with divine purpose and human experience. The Gospels, with their scenes of parables, miracles, and teachings, reveal Jesus not only as a divine shepherd of souls but as a profound advocate for the marginalized. Seen through the lenses of various interpretative approaches, the narratives become allegorical canvases illustrating profound theological tenets that link Jesus' divinity to His radical engagement with poverty.

Interpreting Jesus' interactions with the poor involves a foray into the realms of exegesis, hermeneutics, and socio-historical contexts. Exegetical interpretations focus on direct textual analysis, aiming to uncover the meaning of Jesus' words and actions within their scriptural setting. For instance, when Jesus, in the Beatitudes, declares the poor blessed, it reflects a subversion of contemporary socio-cultural structures, illuminating His ethos as the embodiment of divine compassion. The hermeneutical approach extends beyond textual confines to question the existential implications of Jesus' words for believers across eras, prompting reflections on how Christ's example calls for an active Christian duty to the impoverished.

Socio-historical interpretations offer a lens that grounds the Gospels within the socio-economic dynamics of first-century Palestine. Jesus emerges not just as a celestial figure but as a revolutionary voice in a world riven by inequalities. Analysis of historical texts suggests that His ministry often directed the gaze of His followers upon the least and the lost, inviting a radical reconfiguration of social norms. By dining with tax collectors and touching lepers, Jesus presented a counter-narrative to the prevailing exclusionary practices of His time. These actions are rich with allegorical significance: they hint at the Kingdom of God as an inclusive society where the first are last and the last, first.

On a theological level, allegorical interpretations afford insights into the Christological implications of Jesus' engagement with poverty. Some theologians posit that Jesus' preference for the marginalized serves as a testament to His divine mission. The logion, "The Son of Man has no place to lay His head," becomes more than biographical information; it reflects a deeper theological truth about the incarnation. In becoming poor, Jesus did not merely share the human condition; He sanctified and dignified the state of poverty itself as a path to divine grace. Here, the epistemological overlap between apologetics and social justice becomes evident, portraying Christ's poverty not as a limitation but as a strategic choice that underscores His redemptive purpose.

The allegorical narrative of the Good Samaritan further reinforces this interpretation. It demonstrates through a compelling story how love transcends socio-political boundaries. Jesus, through this parable, embodies divine compassion reaching out to those on the fringes, urging His disciples to similarly break down barriers of division. This act of radical inclusion serves as a poignant theological metaphor for the imago Dei realized in every human being, regardless of social status. It compellingly links the Christian duty of care to apologetic endeavors by embodying the essence of Christ's divine teaching.

Moreover, interpretations that explore the economic parables of Jesus, such as the Parable of the Talents, present a multi-faceted understanding of wealth and responsibility. These narratives don't just convey moral imperatives but also critique systemic inequalities stealthily. Jesus' teachings become an allegory for divine justice, prodding followers to challenge economic disparities and advocate for equitable resource distribution — principles that seamlessly resonate with the guiding ethos of Catholic Social Justice.

In this interpretative exploration, one cannot ignore the symbolic actions of Jesus, which serve as powerful, non-verbal proclamations of His ethos. Take, for example, the cleansing of the Temple. As much as it is a critique of religious corruption, it also symbolizes a societal restructuring that Jesus envisions — a realm where wealth doesn't overshadow worship, and fairness eclipses fanatic legalism. Through such narratives, theological scholars find a rich wellspring from which the Catholic doctrine of the Option for the Poor and Vulnerable draws sustenance.

The nuances revealed through these interpretative approaches provide a profound backdrop for understanding the interconnectedness of social justice and Christological claims. For Roman Catholic theologians and scholars, this interpretative journey evokes Christ's dual identity as both divine and a paradigm of socio-economic solidarity. This theological exploration implores believers to see Christ's example as not merely an ancient blueprint but a perpetual calling intertwined with advocating for the disenfranchised in contemporary contexts.

As we weave these interpretative strands together, a picture emerges where Christ's divinity and His earthly mission create a holistic narrative aligning with the Church's social mission. From exegesis to socio-historical contextualization, each approach uncovers layers of meaning that enrich the discourse on poverty and divinity. Jesus' life becomes a theological symphony that compels a life dedicated to eradicating poverty, reinforcing the notion that advocating for the poor is inherently an apologetic gesture reflecting His divine mandate.

Church Fathers on Social Justice

In the rich tapestry of theological scholarship, the Church Fathers stand as formidable voices echoing through the corridors of history, crafting the mosaic of Christian thought that guides social justice today. Their insights form a bridge between the nascent Church and modern Catholic teaching, illuminating a divine obligation toward those relegated to society's periphery. Rooted in the Gospel's call for compassion and solidarity, these early theologians saw the plight of the poor not merely as a matter for charity but as a profound theological and ethical imperative. Augustine's reflections on earthly cities and heavenly destinies, alongside Chrysostom's fiery homilies on wealth and poverty, reveal a consistent narrative: the Church must engage in an authentic imitation of Christ's love for the marginalized. In their writings, we find the seeds of the Option for the Poor—an enduring principle that calls the faithful to recognize the face of Christ in the least among us. This theological underpinning enhances the apologetic discourse by aligning the Church's social mission with its doctrinal convictions, suggesting that the truth of Christ's divinity is most powerfully affirmed in acts of justice and love.

Early Teachings Within Catholic tradition, the early Church Fathers present a colorful thread of social justice thought that resonates across the ages. Their teachings, while spanning continents and centuries, provide a foundational lens through which the Church's commitment to the poor can be understood—not merely as a moral obligation, but as a theological imperative. Indeed, their voices collectively echo the emphatic cry of a Church seeking to embody Christ's love for the marginalized, a call that reverberates within the modern principle of the "Option for the Poor and Vulnerable."

For the Church Fathers, the question of poverty was not merely an economic or social issue, but fundamentally theological. This understanding is woven into their reflections and treatises, which navigate the precarious intersections of faith, wealth, and generosity. They approached poverty as a tangible reality and a manifestation of spiritual impoverishment, inviting followers of Christ to see in the oppressed a path to encountering the divine itself.

The teachings of the Church Fathers emphasized that material wealth should never eclipse spiritual richness. St. Basil the Great, for instance, offers an allegorical yet poignant illustration: "The bread that you keep belongs to the hungry; the coat kept in your closet, to the naked." Basil's words challenge the faithful to recognize the intrinsic link between material excess and spiritual deficit. To him, generosity was not merely a virtue but a requirement for achieving spiritual wholeness. Through such teachings, early Christians were prompted to confront their attachments to worldly possessions and seek liberation in the communal sharing of God's bounty.

St. John Chrysostom, renowned for his eloquent homilies, offers another compelling narrative. He contended that neglecting the poor was akin to denying Christ himself, a sentiment powerfully expressed in his writings: "If you cannot find Christ in the beggar at the church door, you will not find him in the chalice." Through this statement, Chrysostom suggests that an authentic encounter with the Eucharist is inextricably linked to active engagement with those in need. His exhortations encapsulated the early Church's vision of a justice deeply rooted in worship, urging believers to see acts of mercy as integral to their faith practice.

St. Augustine's thoughts on poverty present yet another dimension, imploring the community to view social inequality through the lens of love and solidarity. He challenges believers to recognize the shared creation in God's image that binds humanity together, irrespective of socioeconomic standing. Augustine asserts that love for one's neighbor is not an abstract ideal but a practical theological necessity. Only through genuine love can the barriers of social stratification be disrupted and rebuilt into bonds of unity and compassion.

In the synthesis of these teachings, the Fathers illuminate a vision of a Church that sees in the plight of the poor an echo of the Crucified Christ. Their insights invite a more profound reflection on the mystery of the Incarnation. By assuming the form of a servant, Christ imbues human suffering with redemptive significance, a reality the Church Fathers believed should inspire Christians to emulate. The paradox of divine poverty thus becomes a clarion call for believers to forsake comfort for the sacrificial love mirrored in Christ's mission.

The early Church Fathers' focus on social justice presents a rich tapestry of theological reflection that remains urgent today. Their writings exemplify a foundational understanding of how economic hardship intertwines with the spiritual journey and how ameliorating suffering becomes a tangible expression of divine love. This theological perspective does not simply offer charity as a remedy for poverty but demands justice as a fundamental component of Christian life.

The resonance of these teachings is both a challenge and an invitation for the contemporary Church. By engaging with the legacy of the Church Fathers, believers are compelled to action, transcending mere passive pity to foster genuine transformation. The Church's mission to seek justice thus emerges not only as a pastoral duty but as a core doctrine that encompasses the entirety of human existence within divine providence.

Such early theological insights continue to inform the modern Catholic tenet of the Option for the Poor, a concept deeply embedded in the Church's social doctrine. The Fathers' perspectives underscore the essential harmony between the pursuit of justice and the confessing of faith in Jesus Christ's divinity. Their teachings encapsulate a profound understanding that spirituality and social justice are not mutually exclusive paths but interconnected dimensions of living the Gospel.

The narratives and exhortations of the Church Fathers, therefore, remain a perennial source of inspiration and guidance. They connect the theological with the tangible, making the plight of the poor not a transient concern but a critical element of the Christian vocation. This synthesis of thought calls believers to cultivate a society marked by equality, compassion, and justice—an earthly reflection of the heavenly kingdom.

In contemplating the early teachings of the Church Fathers, we are invited not only to remember their historical significance but to consider their ever-relevant exhortations. Their witness urges a continuous exploration of how Catholic social teaching can evolve while holding firm to its roots in theological truth. As we navigate modern challenges, their visionary teachings provide the theological heart for a Church dedicated to justice, urging us to love unconditionally, serve humbly, and engage wholeheartedly in the divine mandate of the Gospel.

Chapter 4: Scriptural Basis for Option for the Poor

Within the hallowed texts of the Old and New Testaments, the option for the poor emerges not merely as a theological notion but as a poignant summons to justice and mercy, seeping through the sacred narratives like a river of compassion. From the clarion calls of the prophets, who, in their divinely inspired fervor, demanded justice for the widow and the orphan, to the radical parables of Jesus, depicting the Kingdom of God as one where the last are first, scripture affirms the imperative of preferential love for the marginalized. It is an ethos embedded in the very fabric of divine revelation, where the stories of lepers, tax collectors, and Samaritans upend societal norms, casting the lowly as beloved protagonists in God's redemptive drama. This unmistakable scriptural tradition compels the faithful to recognize Christ himself in "the least of these," urging a commitment that transcends philanthropy, rooting itself deeply in the tenet that the plight of the impoverished is not peripheral but central to the gospel narrative. Indeed, to embrace the option for the poor is to glimpse the divine heart, pulsating with an unyielding love that beckons the Church toward a reflection of Christ's own life and mission.

Old Testament Foundations

In exploring the Old Testament foundations for the principle of the Option for the Poor, one can't help but notice how the texts echo with divine insistence on justice and care for the marginalized. From the laws set forth in Deuteronomy to the passionate cries of the prophets like Amos and Isaiah, there is an unmistakable call for a society where the dignity of every human being—particularly the disadvantaged—is uplifted. The Mosaic Law, with its Jubilee tradition and provisions for the alien, widow, and orphan, forms a moral bedrock that urges believers to not only see justice as a broad, abstract ideal but as a concrete obligation woven into the very fabric of covenantal life. This theological thread runs deep, portraying God's steadfast love and mercy as inseparable from His demand for justice—a dynamic interplay suggesting that to serve the poor is to walk with God Himself. It's a profound glimpse into a divine economy where generosity trumps accumulation and where the community thrives when it cherishes its weakest members. Thus, the Old Testament does more than just anticipate the teaching of Jesus; it establishes a divine mandate for social justice as integral to the life of faith.

Prophetic Literature serves as a crucible in which the molten core of divine justice is poured into the mold of human civilization. Here in the unburnished prose and poetic lamentations of the Old Testament prophets, we encounter an uncompromising insistence on social justice that echoes with the resounding righteousness of God's unwavering concern for the marginalized. The prophets, though often speaking from epochs long past, feel as contemporary as a piercing conscience, embedding themselves into the collective ethos of Catholic social teaching.

The prophets' clarion call for justice pulsates throughout the Old Testament, singing with an urgency that refuses to be stilled by time. Figures such as Isaiah, Jeremiah, and Amos emerge not merely as celestial scribes but as divine advocates, issuing fervent rebuke against the oppressors and offering hope to the oppressed. It is within their words that the concept of the Option for the Poor finds its biblical antecedents, drawing a direct line from the cries of ancient peoples to the structured teachings of the modern Church.

Isaiah, known for his poignant imagery and rhetorical grandeur, presents a vision radically concerned with justice and righteousness. His declarations against the injustices of his time resonate with moral clarity. As he propounds in Isaiah 58:6-7, the true fast God desires is to "loose the chains of injustice" and "share your food with the hungry." This is a prophetic dictum that underlines the ethical imperatives incumbent upon those who align themselves with God's vision of a harmonious society.

Amos, the shepherd-turned-prophet, administers a sobering critique against the societal structures that engendered inequality and exploitation. His words, often searing, echo across time: "Let justice roll down like waters, and righteousness like an everlasting stream" (Amos 5:24). Such imagery propels the prophetic literature into the realm of allegory, representing justice as an unstoppable force that cleanses and renews. Amos's earthy metaphors linger as enduring blueprints for modern advocates of the poor.

Jeremiah, the weeping prophet, immerses his audience in a narrative of imminent judgment and indispensable mercy. His admonitions reveal the heart of God, profoundly troubled by the neglect and abuse of the vulnerable. Yet, Jeremiah also offers a vision of restoration where justice prevails. His insistence on the need for societal conversion forms a crucial pillar in the scriptural basis for the Church's commitment to social justice. The echoes of his prophecies reverberate as a call to both personal and communal transformation.

Micah, known for his succinct summarizations of divine justice, neatly encapsulates the prophetic mission with his well-known exhortation: "to do justice, to love kindness, and to walk humbly with your God" (Micah 6:8). Such a triadic moral code underscores the holistic nature of God's justice, combining action with compassionate intent and humility. This encapsulation not only enlightens the individual but also communities, advocating a societal worldview oriented towards divine law.

Prophetic literature functions not merely as a series of individual pronouncements but rather as a collective testament to the divine insistence on a preferential option for the poor. It maps out the topography of ethical landscape upon which Catholic social teaching builds the edifice of justice. For the prophets, social structures were not immutable objects but were to be examined, critiqued, and, if necessary, dismantled to enforce divine ordinances of equity.

This firm root in prophetic tradition ensures that the Option for the Poor is not an adornment to Catholic doctrine but an integral aspect, woven into the fabric of creation itself. Indeed, the prophets remind us that spiritual health cannot be divorced from social welfare, intertwining theological agenda with social reform. It is through their voices that one discerns the passionate heart of a God who identifies with the suffering and humiliation of the downtrodden.

The prophetic voice, as depicted in the Old Testament, thereby serves as both a mirror and a lamp; it reflects the current state of human inequity while lighting a path toward divine justice. This dynamic finds echoes in contemporary social movements and Catholic teachings, underscoring a perennial truth: the moral commitment to the poor is not only a theological assertion but also a dynamic call to action.

In synthesizing the prophetic literature's ethical exhortations, Catholics and theologians are challenged to enter a living dialogue with the text, one that demands active participation in countering the myriad injustices of the modern world. Not a mere intellectual ascent but a kinetic faith that, inspired by the prophets, seeks to recreate a world where the cries of today's poor are answers through acts of radical love and justice.

Thus, while these ancient writings may appear distant, their call is ever-present. The prophets invite us into a sacred space where divine justice confronts human apathy, challenging us to embody the biblical imperatives for social justice today. Their words endure as a testament to a moral law that does not pass away, forever ensconced within both scripture and tradition as the Option for the Poor – a hallmark of Catholic social ethics embedded within the sacred text's deepest fibers.

New Testament Teachings

The New Testament offers profound insights into the Christian call to prioritize the poor and vulnerable, firmly grounding the option for the poor within the heart of Jesus' mission. Through parables like that of the Good Samaritan and the Beatitudes' teachings, Jesus reframes society's view of wealth, power, and privilege. He consistently elevates the status of the marginalized, emphasizing love and service over material gain. In the Gospel narratives, Jesus aligns himself with those on the outskirts, illustrating a divine ministry underscored by compassion and justice. The apostolic letters further reinforce this, with Paul urging communities to bear one another's burdens, embodying a faith deeply interwoven with acts of mercy. Such teachings call for a radical reorientation towards empathy, mirroring the divine love Christ embodies—a love that advocates for justice and stands unwaveringly with the downtrodden.

Parables of Jesus weave together the intricate threads of New Testament teachings with a tapestry that elevates the principle of the Option for the Poor to profound heights. It's not merely a theological abstraction but a concrete call to action, modeled through the allegories of the Master Teacher himself—Jesus of Nazareth. These parables, succinctly compact yet lush in meaning, invite us to ponder the mysteries of God's kingdom through everyday scenarios. They cast a glaring light upon societal norms and nudge us gently, yet insistently, towards a moral reckoning.

Consider the parable of the Good Samaritan: a tale of compassion as scandalous as it is instructive. In it, Jesus subverts societal expectations by elevating a despised Samaritan as the exemplar of neighborly love, challenging the audience to reconsider who is truly righteous. Here, the narrative not only deflates the false piety cloaked in orthodoxy but delineates an option for the marginalized, those robbed and left to languish by the wayside. Such stories unveil a radical inclusivity written into the DNA of the Gospel, a clarion call for all Christians to align their lives with this paradox of grace over judgment.

Moreover, the parable of Lazarus and the Rich Man paints a stark dichotomy between earthly abundance and spiritual neglect. Lazarus, the beggar at the gate, embodies destitution, often overlooked in favor of the richness of feasts and purple garments. Yet, in the afterlife, the roles are dramatically reversed—a poignant reminder that divine justice eschews worldly standards. Through this tale, Jesus implores his followers to recognize the looming chasm between the prosperous and the poor, challenging them to bridge it with acts of charity and justice.

Jesus' parables possess an uncanny ability to distill complex truths into simple narratives that are at once elusive and direct. The parable of the Sheep and the Goats, for instance, elucidates the eschatological significance of everyday actions towards "the least of these." Acts of kindness done or withheld are revealed as the final test of discipleship, aligning Christian ethic with an unwavering preference for the vulnerable. It's a wake-up call, demanding allegiance to a kingdom where the poor and marginalized are the compass guiding moral and spiritual orientation.

The Sower and the Seeds parable may initially seem like an agrarian lesson. Still, its layers reveal profound depths about receptivity to God's word and the impediments posed by worldly wealth. The thorny ground, choked by life's worries and riches, warns against the seductive allure of material success, hinting at the kingdom values where true prosperity is found in spiritual richness. Such teachings subvert worldly aspirations, envisaging a societal structure where the poor are not just recipients of charity but exemplars of divine favor.

The parables, in their varying forms and complexities, don't just dictate moral imperatives but unfold a vision of the Kingdom of God where the first are last and the last are first. Each story is a gem in the treasury of Gospel literature, offering an epiphanic moment that changes the very nature of what it means to be human and in relationship with others.

They constitute a scriptural foundation for the Catholic Church's Social Teaching, embedding the Option for the Poor deeply within the ethos of Christianity.

Interestingly, these narratives accomplish something that mere didactic proclamations could not—they engage the listener's imagination and moral intuition. By transcending legalistic boundaries, the parables provide a mosaic that delights and provokes, encouraging a dynamic and transformative engagement with the Gospel message. Through their cyclical culmination, they're no mere reiterations but pulsating invitations to live in the complex realm of faith where love for the least becomes the measure of our fidelity to the Incarnate Word.

In a world teetering on the edge of economic inequality and moral indifference, Jesus' parables resurface as essential liturgical texts and provocations for social action. They beckon not just individual conversion but communal transformation, inviting the Church to be the living bread that feeds both spiritually and materially. These stories remind us that the path to holiness runs through the streets of justice and charity, with the poor as our collective guides.

Thus, each parable becomes a refrain in a divine symphony, resonating with a note of urgency—"Do you also go and do likewise." They affirm the indefatigable dignity inherent in each human person, calling for a solidarity that is not token gestures but intentional, sustained, and evangelical. Herein lies the genius of the parables: their simultaneously simple and profound nature compels us towards a faith that is as transformative as it is redemptive, inviting nothing less than a revolution of love.

Chapter 5: Apologetic Support for Jesus' Divinity

In the intricate tapestry of theological discourse, the divinity of Jesus emerges not merely as an article of faith but as a profound testament to the seamless blending of the divine with the human, resonating with the Catholic imperative of empathy for the marginalized. Scriptural evidence, particularly from key Gospel passages, provides an unwavering foundation upon which the apologetic defense of Christ's divinity is constructed. The Gospel narratives, dense with symbolism, portray Jesus not just as an emissary of peace but as the incarnate Logos, embodying both ultimate authority and profound humility. Reflecting on the Christological Councils, such as Nicaea and Chalcedon, we witness an earnest quest for theological clarity that parallels the Church's advocacy for social justice. These councils distilled doctrinal truths, affirming Jesus' divine nature while emphasizing His solidarity with the human plight. Hence, by asserting the sacredness inherent in Christ's very being, the Church implicitly upholds the dignity of the poor and vulnerable, mirroring His compassionate outreach in a modern sociocultural context.

Scriptural Evidence

In exploring the profound linkage between Catholic Social Justice and the divinity of Jesus, the scriptural evidence becomes an illuminating guide, seamlessly weaving theological depth with social advocacy. The Gospels speak with ardent clarity about His divine nature, most notably in John 1:1, where the Logos, the Word made flesh, subsists with God and as God. The synoptic Gospels further narrate instances like the Transfiguration (Luke 9:28-36), offering glimpses of divine glory that affirm His eminence beyond mere humanity. These scriptural affirmations embolden believers, not only in worship but also in the heartfelt task of emulating Christ's compassion in advocating for the least among us. The divine mission, thus, extends into a mandate for social justice, where Christ's preferential care for the marginalized becomes not merely an ethical model but a divine command. This intertwining of scriptural testimony and divine agency invites a reflection on His nature—both profoundly transcendent and intimately present, compelling the Church to advocate ceaselessly for the dignity of the poor and vulnerable, a sacred act that mirrors the divine love enshrined in the Gospel narrative.

Key Gospel Passages provide a rich tapestry of evidence supporting Jesus' divinity, weaving together declarations, miracles, and intimate conversations. Let us begin with the profound opening of the Gospel of John, where the bold proclamation that "the Word was God" (John 1:1) sets the stage for an incarnational narrative. John's theological artistry presents Jesus not merely as a fragmented reflection of the divine but as the very Logos, the eternal principle that not only enlightens but also embodies creation.

In the tapestry of Matthew's gospel, nestled in the harmony of the synoptic tradition, we encounter a moment of divine revelation at the baptism of Jesus. Here, the heavens part, and a voice declares, "This is my beloved Son, with whom I am well pleased" (Matthew 3:17). It's a pivotal juncture, affirming Jesus' unique sonship, which transcends all previous prophetic expectations. This divine endorsement is not an echo from a distant past but a present reality that anchors Jesus' ministry.

Further along, the Transfiguration beckons as a mountain of glory. In this narrative, Jesus' divinity radiates both literally and symbolically as His face shines like the sun, and His clothes become dazzling white (Matthew 17:2). Witnessed by Peter, James, and John, this event heralds Jesus as the fulcrum of the Law and the Prophets, represented by Moses and Elijah. The voice that once parted the heavens at the Jordan now affirms, "Listen to him" (Matthew 17:5), underlining the weight of divine authority that rests upon Him.

A more personal revelation unfolds within the Gospel of John, during an intimate exchange with Philip. When asked to show the Father, Jesus responds, "Whoever has seen me has seen the Father" (John 14:9). This declaration is neither metaphorical nor hyperbolic. It's a concrete reassertion of His consubstantiality with God. The simplicity yet profundity of this statement offers a window into the mystery of the Trinity, blending divinity with the familiarity of the human encounter.

At a cursory glance, the miracles chronicled in the Gospels might appear as acts of compassion or divine favor, yet they also bear a Christological weight. Take for instance Jesus' ability to forgive sins. In Mark, we read, "Son, your sins are forgiven" (Mark 2:5), a pronouncement that stirs theologians and Pharisees alike. Only God can forgive sins, and here lies an implicit assertion of Jesus' divine authority, challenging societal norms and inviting humanity into a transformative relationship with the divine.

Let us not neglect the "I Am" sayings scattered throughout John, reminiscent of God's self-revelation to Moses. Statements like "I am the bread of life" (John 6:35) or "I am the good shepherd" (John 10:11) are laden with theological significance, intertwining identity with divinity. These affirmations do not merely describe a mission or metaphor; they echo the divine identity that beckons a recognition of Jesus' role not just as a teacher or prophet, but as the incarnate God.

Another dimension is witnessed in Jesus' trial before the Sanhedrin, where the High Priest questions Him about His divine claim. In a moment charged with dramatic tension, Jesus declares, "You will see the Son of Man seated at the right hand of Power, and coming with the clouds of heaven" (Mark 14:62). It's a statement veiled in apocalyptic imagery, drawing from the visions of Daniel to assert a divine authority that transcends earthly power structures, confirming His messianic and divine identity. This narrative not only fulfills prophetic vision but also convicts the listener of its veracity through His subsequent resurrection.

The resurrection itself is perhaps the capstone of the divine testament. In the synoptics, women discover the empty tomb, and subsequently, the risen Jesus appears to His disciples, real and tangible. John's gospel amplifies this theme, with Thomas' encounter heightening the emphasis on belief and sight. "My Lord and my God!" (John 20:28) exclaims Thomas, a declaration capturing the essence of Christian faith's transition from doubt to divine affirmation in one breath.

In a narrative intricately woven with theological reflections and parables, the Gospels portray Jesus as a figure of divine empathy, reaching out to the marginalized and the broken. Yet it is His divine nature that gives ultimate authority to His teachings on the preferential option for the poor. The unity of Jesus' divinity and humanity reinforces the Church's mission to see His face in the poor and marginalized, emphasizing that social justice is not merely an ethical imperative but a divine mandate.

Thus, the Gospels do not present mere historical accounts. They unveil a divine drama, where Jesus emerges not only as a herald of the Kingdom but as the fulcrum of divine-human reconciliation. In these passages, believers find not just traditions or lessons, but heartfelt assurances of Jesus' divine nature, beckoning a world grappling with division and advocating a profound call to justice and love. These stories, charged with divine electricity, forever carve paths in the hearts of those who dare to walk in the light of His divinity.

Christological Councils

The Christological Councils, particularly Nicaea and Chalcedon, stand as monumental beacons in the edifice of apologetic support for the divinity of Jesus. These councils, infused with the mellifluous sinews of reason and revelation, sought to elucidate the profound mystery of the Incarnation, uniting divine and human natures in the singular person of Christ. They emerged as responses to heresies that threatened to fragment the nascent faith, articulating truths that serve as the bedrock for both theological inquiry and doctrinal continuity. In these assemblies, the early Church not only defended the divine identity of Christ but also laid a framework that resonates with the Catholic Social Justice teaching of preferring the marginalized. By affirming Christ's full divinity and humanity, the councils underscored the inherent dignity and shared nature of all humanity, echoing a call to uplift those in destitution and align with the Creator's redemptive love. In a paradox as poetic as the parables, these ancient debates elevate our understanding of justice and advocacy, revealing that the acknowledgement of Christ's divinity is intimately woven with a commitment to serve the poorest and the most vulnerable among us.

Nicaea and Chalcedon To fully grasp the emergence of Christological orthodoxy, one must engage with the pivotal moments of the Councils of Nicaea (325 AD) and Chalcedon (451 AD). These were not mere gatherings of ecclesiastical figures, but crucial junctures in which the very essence of Christ's divinity was both challenged and defended, a defense that surreptitiously aligned with the values later encapsulated by Catholic Social Justice. The proceedings and outcomes of these councils provided a robust apologetic support for Jesus' divinity, linking theological affirmations with sociocultural implications.

At Nicaea, the heretical stance of Arianism was the primary opponent. Arius, a priest from Alexandria, propagated the notion that Jesus was a created being, not co-eternal with the Father. The council's response was decisive and eloquent; it issued the Nicene Creed, affirming the consubstantiality (homoousios) of the Son with the Father. This claim was more than a doctrinal stand; it was a declaration of the profound unity and equality among persons of the Trinity, a unity that mirrored the church's vision of social equity and justice. In professing that Jesus was "true God from true God," the council anchored Christ's divinity as a foundation upon which the social principles of justice could squarely rest. Invoking philosophical depth, we might muse that the council's decisions were akin to casting a divine light onto the dark recesses of inequality.

This triumphant proclamation did not emerge untested. The political and theological landscape was a tapestry of tensions, mirroring the societal structures wherein power dynamics often left the poor and vulnerable marginalized. Nicaea's affirmation asserted a theological truth that transcended human hierarchies, positioning the divine nature of Christ as a touchstone for universal dignity and equity, thereby subtly informing the later principles deeming social justice an intrinsic facet of the Christian ethos.

Chalcedon, occurring over a century later, furthered this legacy by addressing the monophysite controversy. When the arguments arose suggesting that Jesus had but a single, divine nature to the exclusion of his human one, the council fathers deployed a nuanced declaration of faith. Their answer, the Chalcedonian Definition, articulated the hypostatic union: that Christ is truly God and truly man, existing in two natures without confusion, change, division, or separation.

This articulation was not a sterile theological postulate. It was an assertion that life through Christ was sanctified in its entirety—divine and human, suggesting a redemptive ethos applicable to both individual and communal existence. The dual nature of Christ speaks allegorically to a call for societal duality, reflecting a harmonious balance between justice and mercy, presaging the option for the poor and vulnerable as a primary conviction in Catholic teaching.

It is fascinating to observe how these Christological affirmations align with social justice imperatives. At Chalcedon, the language of inclusion and clarity outlined boundaries that simultaneously erected bulwarks against oppressive interpretations while offering a reservoir of grace through Christ's nature. The humanity within the divinity of Christ found resonance in the poor's plight, advocating subtly yet powerfully for their defense and upliftment, echoing later in the Church's preferential option for the marginalized.

By solidifying Christ's two natures, the council also reinforced the inherent dignity bestowed upon humanity. If the divine can embrace the human condition, then humanity itself is not only worthy of redemption but deserving of justice. This intertwines elegantly with the Catholic paradigm that positions human dignity at the forefront of its social teachings. Thus, from the acts of Nicaea and Chalcedon emerges a profound moral theology that reverberates through the ages, casting light upon the shadows of history with a call for true equity.

However, this is not merely a historical musings for theologians and scholars. The implications drawn from these councils ripple through the fabric of time, shaping a church committed not just to doctrinal purity but to the living wisdom of service and solidarity. By defending Christ's divinity and his incarnational reality, Nicaea and Chalcedon offered a continuity of faith and action, a binding cord between heaven and earth that Catholic social teachings continue to unravel and reweave into the complex patterns of contemporary society.

These historical councils, then, emerge as both creedal anchors and inexhaustible wells of social wisdom, guiding the Church to act justly, love mercy, and walk humbly with God. In seeking Jesus as truly divine and truly human, Catholic apologetics finds not a division but a convergence, a fusion that empowers believers to address social woes with a foundation rooted in divine justice. Such is the miraculous alchemy wrought by faith, where mysteries of old cast forth innovative beams into future doctrine, shimmering with both immediate and eternal relevance.

Thus, the imperative to understand Nicaea and Chalcedon transcends mere academic curiosity; it demands engagement with the profound implications of Christology upon Catholic Social Justice. The councils presented and solidified truths that not only illuminated theological tenets but also kindled a sacred fire towards advocacy, calling forth the Church to be an unwavering voice for the poor and the marginalized—a testament both to the divinity manifest in Jesus Christ and the dignity residing in every human being.

Chapter 6: Papal Encyclicals on Social Justice

In the rich tapestry of Catholic thought, papal encyclicals serve as both a moral compass and clarion call, weaving timeless truths with contemporary challenges. The encyclical *Rerum Novarum*, marking the dawn of the modern era in 1891, embodies a symphonic convergence of justice and compassion. It unfurls the Church's commitment to the marginalized, setting a precedent that echoes through the corridors of Vatican proclamations to this day. Recent encyclicals have continued this tradition, illuminating social justice issues through a lens polished by doctrinal fidelity and pastoral concern. As they echo themes of human dignity and the inherent worth of each person, these encyclicals stand as bulwarks against the dehumanizing tide of socio-economic disparity. They resonate with the call to an authentic option for the poor, crafted not merely as an ethical obligation but as a testament woven into the divine narrative of Christ's incarnation. In melding advocacy with theological insight, these papal teachings summon the faithful to magnify justice through action rooted deeply in the mystical union of humanity with the divine.

Rerum Novarum and the Modern Era

In the azure dawn of the modern era, the echoes of "Rerum Novarum" resound as a clarion call for justice—enjoining an ancient faith with contemporary reason. This landmark encyclical, promulgated at the cusp of the 20th century, punctuates the Catholic Church's unwavering commitment to social equity, while engaging the tumultuous forces of industrial capitalism and class struggle. Leo XIII, with prophetic insight, articulated a vision that transcends mere economic concerns, harmonizing moral imperatives with the plight of the proletarian soul. The encyclical crystallizes a deep-seated conviction that social justice is not an optional exercise, but a moral mandate—one that stitches the Church's concern for the poor into the very fabric of its doctrinal tapestry. By confronting modern socio-economic dilemmas through the lens of faith, "Rerum Novarum" stitches together the theological threads of Christ's divinity with the Beatitudes' call to righteousness, enfolding a timeless ethos of compassion that insists the sacred and the secular stride hand in hand.

Key Themes Over a century has passed since Pope Leo XIII, in a document both luminous and succinct, addressed the pressing socio-economic issues of his time in the encyclical *Rerum Novarum*. This landmark encyclical, while addressing immediate concerns, laid the foundational bricks for modern Catholic social teaching, establishing principles that continue to echo in the corridors of theological and social discourse.

The encyclical was a clarion call for the Church to engage actively with the issues of capital and labor. It emphasized the dignity of the human person as the cornerstone of all social justice endeavors. This proclamation of human dignity was not merely ethical rhetoric; it was underpinned by the theological assertion that all humans are imago Dei—made in the image of God. In a world often dominated by mechanistic views of labor, the encyclical reinstated the person as the central figure in the social equation.

Rerum Novarum underscored the right to private property, a recognition that human beings, by virtue of their rational nature, have the capability and right to own goods. Yet, this right carries with it the obligation of stewardship, where the use of property should contribute to the common good. Such a dual acknowledgment distinguishes Catholic social teaching from both capitalism and socialism, presenting an alternative grounded in balanced justice.

Coupled with the discourse on property was the earnest emphasis on the rights of workers. In words that resonate as prophetically as they did in 1891, the document calls for fair wages, reasonable working hours, and humane working conditions. This advocacy stands as a testament to the Church's commitment to the 'option for the poor and vulnerable', providing a moral canopy under which the disadvantaged could find shelter.

Furthermore, the encyclical's pervasive theme of subsidiarity insisted that social issues should be addressed at the most immediate level capable of resolving them. This principle not only respects human agency but also champions local and familial involvement over overarching state control. It entrusts power to communities, giving them the ability and responsibility to resolve their internal affairs while calling for assistance from larger institutions only when necessary.

Relating the teachings of *Rerum Novarum* to the modern era, one finds an unyielding relevance. As societies grapple with globalization, technological advances, and economic disparity, the encyclical's themes of human dignity, fair labor practices, and the responsible use of property continue to guide the Church's response to contemporary challenges. The encyclical serves as both a reflection on past injustices and a proactive guide for future social justice endeavors.

Perhaps most intriguing is how these doctrines, centered on the material and immediate, serve a loftier purpose. They act as vessels of divine truth, drawing parallels between the love owed to the poor and the love God embodies in Christ. This connection harmonizes the Church's social mission with its spiritual message, thereby intertwining the apologetic defense of Jesus' divinity with actionable advocacy for social justice. *Rerum Novarum* thus serves a dual function—it awakens the conscience to divine commandments and propels human action towards societal reform.

As we traverse the intricate web of social justice themes within Papal teachings, woven intricately with threads of divine tenets, *Rerum Novarum* emerges as a banner of hope. It is a reminder that the pursuit of social justice is not merely about ameliorating earthly suffering; it is about manifesting the kingdom of God in a world thirsting for redemption. The themes of Leo XIII's encyclical, thus, do not fade with time but pulse with a living urgency as relevant now as they were at their inception.

Recent Papal Documents

In the mosaic of papal teachings, recent documents illuminate the evolving conversation between the Church and the world's pressing social realities. Pope Francis, with his apostolic exhortations and encyclicals like "Evangelii Gaudium" and "Laudato Si'," continues to weave the narrative of compassion for the marginalized and stewardship of creation. These modern writings pronounce a clarion call to integrate faith with tangible action, emphasizing the Church's enduring commitment to social justice. They invite us to discern the divine not just in contemplation but in the cries of the earth and the cries of the poor. These documents are not mere additions to a library of faith but living instruments urging us toward a deeper embodiment of Christ's love for the least among us, nurturing a world where justice and charity walk hand in hand.

Continuity and Development in the discussion of recent papal documents on social justice is a journey from tradition to innovation, a narrative where the past leans forward into the future with a gentle but firm insistence. The continuity is like a river that flows steadily, fed by countless streams of thought, each adding clarity and depth to the discourse on the option for the poor. Papal encyclicals stand as bridges over this river, connecting varied epochs and wisdom distilled through the ages. They are both immutable and adaptive, echoing the voices of the past while responding to the cries of the present.

The encyclicals of recent popes such as John Paul II, Benedict XVI, and Francis don't merely reflect nostalgia for traditional ideals but actively engage with contemporary challenges in a rapidly changing world. The thread of social justice that links these documents is a common tenet, yet it is woven with strands peculiar to each pontificate, addressing unique societal transformations. It is a rich tapestry, a canvas of divine and human encounters.

Consider the vivid imagery painted by Pope John Paul II in "Centesimus Annus." Here continuity manifests not just through doctrinal reiteration but through an empathic dialogue with marginalized communities. The option for the poor isn't merely conceptual; it is incarnate—an embodiment of Christ's ministry on earth. This encyclical invokes the memory of "Rerum Novarum," yet it also dares to dream anew, peering into the face of post-modern poverty and calling for innovation rooted in eternal truths.

Pope Benedict XVI approached the concept of development with a philosophical depth that is characteristic of his theological acumen. In "Caritas in Veritate," he navigates the waters of human dignity and ethical globalization. Development, within this context, is not progression for its own sake but a symbiotic relationship between charity and truth. This encyclical echoes the resounding theme of solidarity across papal teachings but places it within a contemporary landscape, where economic structures are in constant flux.

Yet it is with Pope Francis's "Laudato Si'" and "Fratelli Tutti" that we witness a most profound infusion of continuity and creativity. His encyclicals aren't just documents but manifestos beckoning the global community to adopt a holistic approach to social justice. Francis articulates development not merely as economic upliftment but as an ecological imperative, weaving care for our common home with care for the least among us. It's a clarion call to action, a poetic mandate where continuity demands an active partnership with creation—a divine assignment echoing from Genesis itself.

A critical examination reveals that these recent papal documents don't stand in isolation. They are dialogues with history, orchestrating a symphony from fragments of ancient notes. They are the latest articulations in the Church's living tradition, rooted in but not constrained by what has been. Continuity here doesn't imply stagnation; rather, it suggests a dynamic fidelity that interprets, adapts, and applies age-old wisdom to new existential realities.

Further, the development of these ideas within the encyclicals reflects an ongoing apologetic endeavor—the defense of truths transcending dogmatic statements. There is a harmony between the divine and the humane, a theological anthropology that asserts the dignity of each person as fundamental to any discourse on social justice. Therefore, these documents can be seen as both apologetic and pastoral, providing a robust framework for understanding the Church's commitment to social equity through the lens of divine mercy.

Through this understanding, it becomes clear that the principle of the preferential option for the poor gains momentum over time. It's a rolling wave rather than a static guideline, sweeping through each papal document with renewed vigor. This continuity and development reflect an unyielding fidelity to the Gospel and an evolving response to human suffering.

Each pope, influenced by his specific cultural and historical juncture, contributes a unique perspective to the preferential option for the poor. Such are the threads keeping the Church not only alive but thriving in its mission. While the train of thought is familiar, its journey is propelled by new contexts and demands, inviting a blend of tradition and transformation.

In closing, the recent papal documents exhibit both a reverence for the past and an engagement with the present, achieving a seamless balance between memory and expectation. They remind us that the Church's continuous journey towards social justice is not merely an adherence to ritual but a vibrant testament to the enduring and unfolding mission of the kingdom of God. Through these encyclicals, the message is clear: the Gospel calls us towards a life of charity, solidarity, and hope, compelling the faithful to look outward and embrace a world in flux.

Chapter 7: Councils and Social Doctrine

In much the same way a mosaic reveals its intricate design through the placement of each individual piece, the councils of the Church have historically provided the cohesive frameworks that merge theology with social advocacy. The Second Vatican Council, a luminary amidst the epochs of church history, reinvigorated the ethos of Catholic social doctrine. Through its seminal documents, it beckoned the faithful toward a renewed commitment to social justice, urging an active engagement with the worldly struggles of poverty and inequality. This council, with its profound emphasis on aggiornamento—or the bringing up to date—did not merely affirm the preferential option for the poor, but intertwined such imperative with the divine mission espoused by none other than Christ Himself. In the ongoing narrative that has unfolded since Vatican II, subsequent encyclicals and declarations have diligently amplified this call for justice, portraying it not as a charitable choice but as an evangelical necessity. Thus, the councils, with their doctrinal pronouncements, serve as both compass and clarion, directing the Church toward its immutable calling of embodying Christ's compassion in a fractured world.

Vatican II and Social Advocacy

The Second Vatican Council, or Vatican II, marked a seismic shift in the Church's engagement with social justice, crafting a new paradigm of advocacy that married timeless truths with contemporary issues. This pivotal moment revealed the Church's deepened commitment to the principle of the Option for the Poor, aligning ecclesiastical authority with the urgent cries for human dignity and justice resonating across the world. Key documents like "Gaudium et Spes" outlined a vision where the Church becomes a beacon of hope, actively engaging in the alleviation of poverty and in casting light into the shadows of human suffering. By broadening the lens through which faith and reason apply to modern society, Vatican II's teachings implore Catholics to not only reflect on the divine mysteries but to animate these revelations into acts of love and justice, resonating with the apologetic mission of proclaiming Christ's divine compassion. Amidst a world fraught with unrest, Vatican II's clarion call for social advocacy weaves a tapestry where the sacred and the secular converge, inviting the faithful to pursue not just a heaven above, but a justice on earth.

Major Documents Vatican II, a pivotal council in the annals of the Roman Catholic Church, brought with it a prolific outpouring of documents that underscored an invigorated commitment to social advocacy. These documents, galvanized by the spirit of aggiornamento—renewal and updating—transcended conventional ecclesiastical boundaries to call the Church towards a renewed engagement with the world's social and economic realities. At the heart of this endeavor was the notion that faith and daily life were not disjointed realms, but intimately intertwined tapestries of human experience.

Perhaps no document better encapsulates this sentiment than the pastoral constitution *Gaudium et Spes* ("Joy and Hope"). A landmark in ecclesiastical writing, it articulated a vision of the Church as both a beacon of hope and a participant in addressing the complex issues of the modern world. This text elevated human dignity, emphasizing that the Church's mission couldn't be isolated from the plight and aspirations of humanity. *Gaudium et Spes* sought to speak to every person, extending beyond the traditional ecclesial audience to embrace all of humanity, resonating with the inclusive love espoused by Christ himself.

Complementing this text was *Nostra Aetate*, a declaration that signified an epochal shift in the Church's approach to other religions. Its few pages were revolutionary in outlook, advocating not for isolation but for dialogue, understanding, and mutual respect. In a world marred by division, the document proposed a path of unity through acknowledgment and appreciation of diversity. By fostering an empathy-driven narrative, the Church positioned itself as a catalyst for comity in the global arena, truly living up to the call of loving one's neighbor, irrespective of creed.

Moreover, the decree *Apostolicam Actuositatem* empowered the laity to assume a dynamic role in social advocacy. Moving beyond the traditional confines of clerical initiative, this document recognized that the lay faithful, imbued with the same Spirit, could actively partake in the Church's mission to transform and uplift society. By valorizing the vocation of the laity in world affairs, the Council acknowledged that social justice was not merely the province of the ordained but a universal call to action for every believer.

Dignitatis Humanae, another key document, constructed a robust defense of religious freedom. Here, the Council affirmed that coercion was antithetical to genuine faith, advocating for individuals' right to spiritual self-determination. This was not merely a recognition of liberty but an affirmation of conscience as a sacred sanctuary. In a world often plagued by oppression, this declaration of freedom positioned the Church as a guardian of the inherent dignity of every individual.

These documents collectively form the backbone of Vatican II's social advocacy, sculpting a renewed ecclesial image—one that is proactive in addressing the societal complexities of the era. They chart a course for the Church, encouraging it to embody both faith and reason, justice and mercy, orthodoxy and action. Yet, these writings are not static relics but living documents, meant to be engaged with, reinterpreted, and implemented as society evolves.

The aspects of social advocacy highlighted by these Vatican II documents share an intrinsic alignment with the principle of the Option for the Poor and Vulnerable, which permeates the broader landscape of Catholic Social Teaching. This principle calls for a prioritization of the needs of society's most marginalized, echoing the gospel's call to be a voice for the voiceless, a defender of the defenseless. In this way, the Church aligns itself with Christ's own mission to proclaim good news to the poor and liberation to the oppressed.

This synergy between the Council's pronouncements and foundational Catholic doctrines underscores a deeper theological ethos. The interconnectedness is not merely strategic but deeply philosophical, reflecting a vision of divine love manifest in temporal acts of charity and justice. Vatican II envisioned a Church that was indeed universal—catholic in the truest sense—pouring itself out in service to the least of these as an act of worship and testimony to Christ's divinity.

As we reflect on these seminal texts, they invite ongoing dialogue within the Church—to listen, to learn, and to act. They call for a Church that reads the signs of the times, discerning where God is at work and joining in that sacred task. In doing so, the Council's documents reassure us that the heart of the Church beats in rhythm with the joys and hopes, the griefs and anxieties, of the people it seeks to serve and transform.

Vatican II's clarion call is thus twofold: it is an affirmation of the Church's divine mandate to proclaim the mystery of faith and a recognition of its earthly mission to embody that faith in actions of love and justice. The documents remain a testament to a historic moment when the Church gazed outward and inward, reimagining its role in a world replete with challenges and opportunities.

In the end, these writings don't just bear witness to a moment in history but invite participation in an ongoing narrative—a story of divine love that unfolds through the lived reality of community, advocacy, and mission accompanying humanity with the whisper of God's enduring promise. Vatican II, through its major documents, challenges the believer: to embrace an ever-widening circle of care and concern, to see the divine in the humble acts of justice we bring to life around us.

Post-Vatican II Developments

In the aftermath of Vatican II, a luminous dawn broke over the Church, awakening a profound engagement with social justice and accentuating the Option for the Poor as an intrinsic expression of ecclesial identity. The clarion call of the Council echoed through the Church's halls, reverberating in encyclicals and declarations that married the mystical with the mundane, a symphony of doctrine and discourse. This era witnessed the Church stepping into the modern world, not with timidity but with the profound confidence of a shepherd tending to his flock. It demonstrated an unwavering commitment to social advocacy, a manifestation of the divine Word incarnated amid temporal struggles. The melding of doctrinal depth and social outreach post-Council served as both a beacon and a bridge, harmonizing the Church's eternal truths with the transient needs of humanity. Through these developments, the Church articulated a narrative where the fullness of Christ's divinity was exemplified in its unwavering option for the marginalized, thereby unveiling a path of justice as a sacred pilgrimage towards the Divine.

Encyclicals and Declarations following the Second Vatican Council represent a turning point, embodying an energetic synthesis of faith and reason, mercy and justice. The church, confronted by the storms of modernity, did not retreat; rather, it leaned forward, listening and pondering as the world spoke in a thousand tongues. Here, in the symphony of words written by successive pontiffs, echoes the imperative of the human heart molded in the image of divine love. *Gaudium et Spes* and its prophetic foresight established the blueprint, mapping the contours of future pronouncements with courage and clarity.

In tracing this path, one cannot overlook the prolific contributions of John Paul II, whose encyclicals *Sollicitudo Rei Socialis* and *Centesimus Annus* boldly reasserted the profound connection between Christ's teachings and social responsibilities. At the heart of these texts is the indelible conviction that every human life has innate dignity. John Paul II tirelessly emphasized a preferential love for the poor, a cornerstone of the church's social doctrine, reflecting the salvific mission of Christ.

Sollicitudo Rei Socialis cast an unflinching gaze upon the structures of sin that perpetuate injustice, echoing the cry of the oppressed through its unwavering call for solidarity. In evocative passages, it sketches a world caught between the pincers of excess and deprivation, urging the faithful to harness the transformative power of compassion as a force for change. It's not a simple exhortation—it's a call to live out a radical synthesis of faith infused with action.

Meanwhile, *Centesimus Annus* marks a centennial reflection on *Rerum Novarum*, confidently revisiting and updating the church's witness as guardian of authentic human development. Where earlier missives might have withstood the tide, this document wades into the flux, reconstructing and reaffirming the inviolable dimensions of social justice. Its passages often unravel like conversations, bridging past tradition and present need, engaging with a world steeped in the ambitions of the market while reminding it of its moral obligations.

Benedict XVI, with the encyclical *Caritas in Veritate*, delved into the interplay of truth and love, asserting the timeless connection between ethical conduct and ecclesiastical authority. This document broadens the scope of Catholic social thought, introducing ethics into economic and political discourse and deftly critiquing entrenched models of growth and progress. It posits that true development must be rooted in charity guided by truth, a notion with vast implications for how societies delineate justice and foster welfare.

Pope Francis, too, brings his unique voice to the dialogue through *Evangelii Gaudium* and *Laudato Si'*, marrying the realities of poverty with environmental advocacy. He extends the church's moral compass to encompass not only human relationships but also humanity's connection with creation. His writing bursts with imagery and urgency as he pleads for a church that is poor and for the poor. Francis' approach is an invitation to a holistic conversion, reconciling all of creation under the banner of shared stewardship and mutual respect—a symphony of care for both the earth and its inhabitants.

These encyclicals and declarations reflect not just responses to societal changes but embody theological development grounded in lived reality. They serve as compasses for modern Catholics, urging communities not merely to engage in charitable acts but to advocate for systemic change within their societies. The church, through these powerful proclamations, functions as both healer and catalyst, bridging the chasm between doctrine and lived experiences.

These writings don't stand in isolation—they are part of a greater narrative threaded through the church's mission to affirm the divine image in every person. The declarations and encyclicals are imbued with the spirit and teachings of Christ, emphasizing not just belief but active participation in the redemption of the world. They bid the faithful to see the face of Christ in the marginalized and to live as beacons of hope in the shadows of hardship.

Thus, as one stands on the shoulders of these giants, the mandate is clear: the work of social justice entwined with the defense of Christ's divinity is not disparate but innately linked. These encyclicals serve as bridges, closing the gap between theological ideas and the tangible realities of everyday life, inviting all to weave their unique voices into the ongoing hymn of salvation history. Through comprehension and commitment, each becomes a note in the divine harmony, a testament to the unity of truth, love, and justice.

Chapter 8: Integrating Theology and Advocacy

When theology marries advocacy, the union births a vibrant tapestry where enduring truths weave into the fabric of societal transformation. This integration isn't merely academic—it beckons us to examine the deep harmony between the miraculous claims of Jesus' divine nature and the church's preferential love for the marginalized. Such an alliance demands both a profound introspection of faith and its tangible application in the world. Faith, like a seed, germinates in the loam of reality, insisting that the theological musings of hope and redemption manifest as concrete action towards justice. It's as though the Gospel's spiritual nourishment is only complete when shared with those beleaguered by the world's inequities. Here, the scholar and the activist find common ground, their pursuits converging as one divine mission to illuminate paths out of darkness. Faith, indeed, without such works, would remain a silent song, yearning to echo in the hearts of both the faithful and the forlorn.

Theological Reflections

At the heart of integrating theology and advocacy lies a profound intertwining of faith and action, where the Word takes flesh not just in belief, but in the beatitudes of daily life. Catholic Social Justice, with its defining option for the poor and vulnerable, does not merely present a call to charity, but an invitation to embody divine empathy—a mosaic of compassion reflecting the very nature of Jesus Christ, whose divinity is defended through apologetics. Here, theology becomes allegory; standing as a lantern of hope, it illuminates the world to the transformative power of grace and justice. Just as the Incarnate Christ walked among us, taking on human fragility, so does the Church feel compelled to walk alongside those on the margins. The philosophical and spiritual underpinnings of this journey remind us that in advocating for justice, we do not drift from theological orthodoxy but draw nearer to its source, revealing the sacred in the mundane and the divine in our common humanity.

Systematic Approaches As we endeavor to weave the rich tapestry of Catholic theology with the threads of social advocacy, one cannot overlook the necessity of methodical approaches that ground our efforts. Systematic approaches in integrating theology and advocacy begin with a deep dive into the intricacies of theological reflections. Such reflections serve as the cornerstone, creating a cohesive structure that allows for meaningful engagement with the world's pressing social issues.

Our journey begins with the foundational principle of Catholic theology: the divine dignity of each human person as a reflection of God's image. In this light, the option for the poor and vulnerable emerges not simply as a charitable notion but as a theological imperative. Systematic theology provides a framework that identifies social justice as a core tenet intertwined with the essence of Christology. Here, the incarnation itself—God becoming human—becomes a profound statement of solidarity with the marginalized. By embracing humanity in its entirety, Christ sets a model for believers to follow, compelling them to exist in active support of those on society's peripheries.

The dynamic interplay between apologetics and social justice also requires systematic examination. In apologetics, the defense of Jesus' divinity must go beyond theoretical discourse to include practical manifestations of divine love. The historical councils and scriptural exegeses provide robust defenses of Christ's nature, yet the true testament to His divinity is borne out in actions of grace and mercy. The task of theology is thus to harmonize doctrinal clarity with ethical obligation, fostering a robust faith that naturally extends into advocacy.

Stepping deeper into this conversation, the methodologies employed by systematic theologians are crucial. At the heart of this dialogue lies a hermeneutical approach that seeks to interpret the signs of the times through the lens of scriptural and doctrinal insights. Theological reflections steeped in the history of the Church's social teachings can guide believers in deciphering contemporary realities. It is here that systematic approaches provide a scaffold upon which believers can construct their understanding of social justice, rooted deeply in doctrinal truths.

Historical theology offers another layer of systematic approaches as it chronicles the Church's evolving understanding of social advocacy. Each epoch of Church history brings forth new insights and methodologies for addressing poverty and injustice. The systematic study of these developments reveals a tradition that, while deeply rooted in biblical exegesis and patristic wisdom, remains adaptable to the current socio-economic climate. This adaptability is essential for theology to remain relevant, allowing it to generate advocacy strategies that resonate with contemporary audiences.

In crafting these approaches, an understanding of ecclesiology—the study of the Church— becomes vital. The Church, as a collective body of believers, acts as a beacon of hope and transformation. Systematic theology explores how this body can institutionalize social justice as part of its mission, encouraged by the teachings of Vatican II and subsequent papal encyclicals. By systematically linking Church teachings to advocacy efforts, believers are equipped not just to articulate their faith, but to act upon it, propelling the mission from contemplation to tangible action.

The engagement of laity further extends the reach of these systematic approaches. It underscores the notion that advocacy is not confined to clergy but is the responsibility of every believer. By educating and inspiring the laity through theological reflections, the Church empowers a new generation of advocates. This democratization underscores the notion that the pursuit of justice is an integral part of living out one's faith. Systematic approaches provide the necessary theological scaffolding to ensure that this endeavor is both grounded and guided by the tenets of the faith.

Close examination of systemic structures within society also plays a pivotal role. A theologically informed critique of socio-economic systems allows for a more profound engagement with the causes of inequality. Systematic theology, by contextualizing these critiques within the broader narrative of salvation history, envisions a transformative impact on societal structures. It posits that advocacy, rooted in robust theological thought, possesses the power to not only respond to injustice but to reform systems in alignment with the Gospel.

Through the systematic study of these intersections, theology moves beyond mere academic exercise; it becomes an embodied praxis, a lived reality that echoes the incarnational aspect of Christianity. Systematic approaches, when implemented, result in a praxis deeply enmeshed with the lived experiences of the poor and marginalized, offering both theological insights and practical solutions.

Systematic approaches emphasize the need for continuity in action and contemplation, forging a path that leads from theological insights to practical implications. It recognizes that true advocacy is born from a dynamic and ongoing engagement with both scripture and the lived experiences of the faithful. By integrating systematic methodologies with theological reflections and advocacy, one embarks on a journey of transforming theology into a living, breathing force for justice.

Social Action Implications

In the intricate dance between theology and advocacy, the implications for social action are profound and transformative. When the Church takes its theological convictions about the divinity of Christ and marries them to the imperative of advocating for the poor, it doesn't just preach— it acts. This confluence compels believers to scrutinize societal structures through a dual lens: the sacred vision of Christ's incarnate love and the unyielding call for justice. As advocates, Roman Catholics find themselves not merely adherents of doctrine but artisans of the Kingdom, shaping reality in a way that reflects the divine preference for the marginalized. Such integration insists on a praxis where faith is enacted not solely within sacred walls but in the marketplaces and alleyways, wherever human dignity is threatened. Thus, the call to action becomes a moral syllogism, where the ultimate truth of Christ's divinity inexorably leads to the sacramental reality of serving 'the least of these,' reshaping both the world and the hearts of those within it.

Practical Guidelines flow naturally from the realization that theology and advocacy are not mere companions but are inherently intertwined. The theological premise of integrating the divinity of Jesus with the call for social justice through the lens of the Church's preferential option for the poor invites profound reflection and practical application. Understanding these dual commitments requires not just an intellectual assent but an activation of those beliefs into the lived realities of individuals and communities. To truly embody these principles necessitates that we, as Catholic practitioners and advocates, engage in more than theoretical discussions; we must enter the world of action, aligning our deeds with our creeds.

At the heart of the integration lies the belief that every action, whether grand or small, should mirror the compassion and love exhibited by Christ. The practical outworking of this belief begins with personal transformation. It's essential that each individual deeply engages with the Scriptures, thus allowing them to illuminate and inform contemporary social challenges. Recognizing the Word as a living testament that cries out for justice ensures that theological contemplation remains connected to the existential needs faced by our communities today.

To operationalize these guidelines, one must strive to establish an inner consistency between one's theological convictions and their sociopolitical engagements. Consider the impact of aligning daily choices with theological understandings of social justice—choices in how one consumes, how one votes, and how one extends generosity. While such acts might appear mundane, they ripple across the broader tapestry of societal norms. Thus, practical theology demands an intentional audit of personal and communal practices, aligning them with the justice-oriented blueprint set forth by the Gospel.

Another layer of practicality involves education and catechesis. The community, both within the Church and beyond, must be nourished with robust theological education that underscores the interconnection between advocating for social justice and honoring the divine in Christ. This education should aim to dismantle any perceived dichotomies between spiritual salvation and temporal liberation, urging believers towards a holistic approach that synthesizes both.

The Church's role as a beacon for social justice cannot be understated. Parishes and dioceses should foster environments that encourage the laity to engage in social action initiatives. Formulating programs that place theology in action—whether through service projects, advocacy groups, or interfaith collaborations—can catalyze genuine change. Encouraging lay participation in these initiatives allows for the democratization of theology, bringing it out from the confines of academia or clerical authority and placing it within the hands and hearts of ordinary people.

Incorporating the preferential option for the poor within advocacy initiatives necessitates deliberate outreach. This might look like building partnerships with grassroots organizations or non-profits that align with these Catholic commitments. Engaging with those at the margins requires not only material aid but an authentic relationship-building approach that respects and uplifts the dignity of each person. Encountering Christ in the face of the marginalized further enriches theological understanding and guides the Church's advocacy efforts.

Perhaps one of the most challenging yet critical aspects of these practical guidelines involves the prophetic task of challenging structures of sin and injustice. The Church, called to be a voice for the voiceless, must navigate the tension between being a mediator of peace and an advocate for justice. This calls for courage in public witness—speaking truth to power and refusing complacency in the face of inequity. Engaging with policymakers, participating in rallies, and using platforms to shed light on injustices are pivotal actions that must emerge from steadfast theological commitment.

The discourse surrounding integrating theology and advocacy must also address sustainability and accountability. Developing rigorous frameworks that ensure initiatives are not only effective but also ethical is crucial. This involves setting measurable outcomes and regularly revisiting the effectiveness of advocacy strategies. By doing so, these initiatives remain dynamic and responsive to evolving societal needs, always staying rooted in foundational theological principles.

Lastly, the journey of advocacy and justice is not a solo endeavor but a collective pilgrimage. As such, networking with wider Catholic and interfaith communities strengthens advocacy efforts. These relationships enrich the Church's capacity to respond to social needs comprehensively and creatively. Dialogue across diverse theological and socio-cultural contexts furthers solidarity and draws upon shared values, creating a more extensive and unified front against injustice.

In summary, the practical guidelines for integrating theology and advocacy insist upon a seamless connection between belief and action. Engaging in personal transformation, fostering educational programs, building community initiatives, challenging injustices, ensuring sustainable practices, and developing interfaith collaborations pave the way for a living theology that speaks into the world. Thus, our mission is not only to ponder the mysteries of the divine but to let those mysteries animate our pursuit of justice, mercy, and love.

Chapter 9: Contemporary Social Issues within Catholic Doctrine

The modern tapestry of society reveals a complex interplay of challenges and opportunities, particularly when examined through the lens of Catholic doctrine. In our time, the Church encounters pervasive issues such as global poverty and systemic injustice, demanding a response rooted deeply in its enduring teachings. While these problems are as old as humanity itself, the Church harnesses novel initiatives and responses, both locally and globally, to create pathways for hope and justice for the marginalized. The principle of the option for the poor and vulnerable echoes through these endeavors, serving as a moral compass that aligns with the divine call exemplified in the life and ministry of Jesus Christ. By addressing these issues not merely as policy concerns but as profound spiritual and moral imperatives, Catholics are urged to see the face of Christ in the suffering. Herein lies the powerful juxtaposition of contemporary social advocacy with the timeless gospel message: a challenge to rise beyond mere obligation towards transformational love and justice. Through a faithful reflection of these principles in action, the Church not only speaks but embodies the gospel today, continually bridging ancient truths with modern exigencies.

Global Poverty and Injustice

Pondering the intertwining paths of global poverty and injustice within the Catholic doctrine brings us face to face with the illusory boundaries that seem to separate the spiritual from the temporal. At the heart of Catholic social teaching lies the principled option for the poor and vulnerable, a commitment that implores us to see Christ's divinity manifested in every act of justice. This doctrine challenges us to act—transcending mere empathy and entering into a realm of profound solidarity with those living in destitution. Here, faith and apologetics unite in a luminous dance; poverty is not just a social ill to be alleviated but a divine invitation to embody Christ's love in action. As we engage with global injustices, these moral imperatives beckon us to recognize that our spiritual salvation is entwined with our pursuit of justice for the marginalized, forging an apologetic narrative that asserts Jesus' divinity not solely through theological discourse but through lived compassion that resounds across nations. This synergy reveals the potency of faith as both a transformative and unifying force, compelling adherents to rise above indifference and influence the world stage with compassionate advocacy.

Case Studies The complex tapestry of global poverty and injustice weaves through the fabric of many societies, a poignant reflection of enduring struggles. In this section, we'll explore specific instances where Catholic doctrine intersects with these challenges, revealing the profound influence of the Church's teachings on both the afflicted and the advocates.

Consider the Philippines, a predominantly Catholic nation grappling with extreme poverty. Amidst natural calamities and economic disparities, an inspiring narrative unfolds—a story of resilience shaped by faith. Here, the Catholic Church plays a pivotal role in uplifting the destitute, echoing the imperative of the 'Option for the Poor.' Church-led initiatives like feeding programs and microfinance projects provide not just immediate relief but also sustainable futures for many. The Church's approach, deeply rooted in solidarity with the impoverished, exemplifies the doctrine's living practice. It reflects a theological engagement with societal woes, extending beyond charity to advocate for structural changes.

In contrast, let's turn our gaze to Brazil, where liberation theology found fertile ground amidst vast economic inequality and social injustice. The commitment to the poor wasn't merely an abstract principle; it was a movement. Priests and laypeople engaged directly in political activism, challenging systemic injustices that perpetuated poverty. This intersection of faith and activism highlighted the potential of Catholic theology to act as a catalyst for societal transformation. The Church in Brazil not only preached the gospel but incarnated it in service and advocacy, raising poignant questions about justice, human dignity, and divine love.

On another continent, the African experience, particularly in regions like the Democratic Republic of Congo, adds a rich layer to our understanding. Here, amidst conflict and deprivation, the Church's mission has been one of accompaniment, standing with communities ravaged by war and disenfranchisement. Catholic schools and hospitals become sanctuaries, offering education and healthcare as tangible manifestations of hope. They do more than address physical needs; they restore dignity and foster peace, illustrating how doctrinal principles can inspire practical, life-affirming action.

The role of Catholic Relief Services (CRS) further underscores this commitment. Operating in over 100 countries, CRS endeavors to alleviate poverty and promote justice, embodying the Church's call to serve 'the least of these.' Through innovative agricultural programs in Ethiopia and emergency relief in Syria, CRS exemplifies a global application of Catholic social teaching, affirming the intrinsic worth of every human life while championing sustainable development and peace-building efforts.

These case studies reveal a profound synergy between Catholic social doctrine and apologetic theology. The defense of Jesus' divinity finds seamless integration with the Church's mission towards the marginalized. Just as Christ's incarnation is a divine affirmation of human dignity, the Church's work among the impoverished signals a continual incarnation, bringing the gospel's truth to bear on the world's pains.

In India, where caste dynamics intertwine with poverty, the Church's presence becomes a testament of radical inclusivity. Catholic missionaries, through education and health services, challenge oppressive structures, raising the marginalized to new heights of opportunity and freedom. Their pragmatic work, buoyed by a theological commitment to justice, illustrates how distinct facets of Catholic teaching converge to address contemporary issues.

Yet, challenges remain. Critics argue about the effectiveness and motivations behind some philanthropic efforts. In many instances, questions arise about whether charitable acts perpetuate dependency or genuinely foster empowerment. These critiques push the Church to continually reassess its methods, ensuring that its mission aligns with authentic human development rather than a mere palliative endeavor.

In urban settings across North America, Catholic initiatives confront homelessness and hunger. Parish-based programs and nonprofits, such as St. Vincent de Paul societies, embody the Church's commitment to neighborly love, transcending mere rescue operations to grapple with systemic issues like affordable housing and living wages. The engagement with policymakers and community leaders illustrates a strategic approach to social justice, rooted in faith yet forward-thinking in execution.

Ultimately, these case studies provide a window into the practical outworking of Catholic social teaching on global poverty and injustice. Each example, distinct in its context yet unified in purpose, challenges us to conceive theology not as static doctrine but as a dynamic force compelling change in the world. Herein lies a shared journey—a mutual endeavor to realize a more just world, inspired by the divine call to love and serve.

Church Responses

In navigating the ever-shifting landscapes of contemporary social issues, the Catholic Church finds itself wielding both age-old wisdom and the impetus for renewal. Rooted in a doctrine that strives to uplift the least among us, the Church's responses integrate theological tenacity with palpable advocacy, echoing the heartbeat of the divine yet resonating with the cries of the marginalized. Through recent initiatives, such as those undertaken by Caritas Internationalis and inspired by papal encyclicals like "Laudato Si'" and "Fratelli Tutti," the Church challenges social apathy and addresses systemic injustices. Its endeavors are not merely temporal interventions but manifestations of an eternal mandate: to embody Christ's love in every corner of the world. By aligning with a theology that values both truth and compassion, the Church endeavors to sow seeds of justice that will bear fruits of dignity and hope for the poor and vulnerable, standing as a testament to the symphony between orthodoxy and praxis. The bedrock of these efforts remains a balance between heartfelt homilies and purposeful action, echoing the apostles' call to live a faith that sings with justice while upholding the divinity that underpins and propels its mission.

Recent Initiatives The Catholic Church's response to contemporary social issues is like a kaleidoscope of initiatives that continuously shift, reflecting the changing patterns of our world's urgencies. One cannot ignore the profound effort this ancient institution makes in steering its lengthy history towards engaging meaningfully with today's dilemmas. This section will weave together the strands of these recent endeavors, highlighting not only their scope but also their impact on global consciousness.

The beating heart of the Church's recent initiatives often finds itself in the depths of poverty relief, a cause as old as the Church itself. Today, more than ever, this mission is critical. Across continents, the Catholic Church, through numerous programs, addresses the material needs of the poor, perhaps embodying the Beatitudes as living catechism. In Africa and Asia, the commitment to sustainable agriculture projects helps local communities not only survive but thrive. These projects underscore a shift from mere charity to empowerment, a testament to the evolving understanding that dignity and self-sufficiency are crucial for genuine alleviation of poverty.

Pope Francis's papacy has been a beacon of activist spirituality, sparking a series of fresh initiatives designed to emphasize both human dignity and environmental stewardship, the twin pillars of his seminal encyclical "Laudato Si'." Crafting a dialogue between theology and sustainability, the Church has invested in educational programs aimed at raising awareness of environmental issues, urging a symbiotic relationship with our planet. This approach respects the intrinsic link between caring for the Earth and caring for the poor, who are invariably the first to suffer from environmental degradation.

The Vatican has not remained silent on the subject of migration and refugee crises perpetuating around the globe. Recent initiatives have been geared towards advocacy and direct aid. Caritas Internationalis, the Church's main charitable arm, embarks on missions supporting displaced populations, providing food, shelter, and legal assistance. The theology of hospitality is vividly enacted as the Church becomes a sanctuary for the marginalized and the displaced, echoing its call to see every human being as bearing the image of Christ himself.

In the sphere of health initiatives, the Church has broadened its reach, especially during the global COVID-19 pandemic. Catholic hospitals and clinics around the world have been at the forefront of providing medical care and support. Campaigns for equitable vaccine distribution have been vigorous and vocal, making the cries for justice not just a matter of faith but of pragmatic necessity. The Church's advocacy for the vulnerable doesn't taper within the confines of ecclesial responsibilities but extends its branches into the exigencies of global public health.

Education has also been a significant focus of the Church's recent initiatives. Modern-day scholars endeavor to transform Catholic education to better address contemporary issues of social justice and inclusivity. Curricula are being redesigned to integrate Catholic social teachings more comprehensively, ensuring that emerging generations are well-versed in moral reasoning and advocacy. This transformation acts not just as an ivory tower reflection of doctrinal ideals but as a practical blueprint for engaging with real-world challenges.

The Catholic Church, compelled by its doctrine of universal love and justice, operates in myriad ways across the globe, seeking to mend the fractures of societal sins. Recent interfaith dialogues have sought to bridge divides, fostering a communal vision of peace and cooperation between diverse religious traditions. These efforts reflect a deep-seated recognition that contemporary social issues transcend any single belief system and require concerted, unified responses. Such endeavors help create platforms for shared values, emphasizing the universal principles of dignity, compassion, and justice—a triptych upon which the benevolence of humanity can be unfolded.

Yet, alongside these laudable initiatives, the Church continually confronts the challenge of articulating its role in a world that is often skeptical of institutions. Its endeavor finds resonance in community-focused projects, where ecclesiastical authority partners with local agencies, creating symphonies of cooperation that echo the Holy Trinity's relational essence. Whether through urban food banks or rural vocational training, these localized efforts contribute to a mosaic of sustainable development—an embodiment of the Gospel imperative to love thy neighbor.

Therein lies the allegory: beneath the grand façades of basilicas, sanctity is not just housed in gold-leafed chapels but reflected in the hands of those serving meals in soup kitchens or drafting policies in boardrooms aimed at reducing economic disparity. Through this allegorical lens, the Church's recent initiatives are seen not merely as acts of charity but as incarnations of divine will, seeking to sanctify the secular through engagement and empathy.

Perhaps one of the most poignant developments is the Church's growing acknowledgment of the voices from its periphery—lay people, particularly women, who have been crucial architects in these initiatives. Emphasizing co-responsibility for the Church's mission, recent initiatives reflect this broader, inclusivist ethos. In this light, the synodal process has begun to draw attention, seeking to harness the collective wisdom and experience of the entire Catholic community in addressing modern-day challenges.

While strategies may vary, the underlying essence of the Church's initiatives rests upon an enduring philosophical premise: social justice is inseparable from faith. As a sapling's roots intermingle with the soil, nourished by its surroundings, so is Catholic doctrine enriched by action, finding its truest expression not in the austerity of silence but in the fervor of deeds. With these initiatives, the Church not only responds to contemporary social issues but invites a rethinking of its role—ever ancient, yet ever new—in the world it seeks to serve.

Chapter 10: Linking Apologetics and Social Justice

In the rich tapestry of Catholic thought, the threads of apologetics and social justice interweave, revealing a harmonious pattern where theology meets advocacy. This chapter endeavors to bridge these seemingly disparate realms by exploring the intricate dance between the divine mission of Christ and the Church's call to uplift the marginalized. At the heart of this connection lies a shared commitment to truth and justice, resonating with the principle of the Option for the Poor and Vulnerable that echoes Christ's own ministry. Apologetics serve not only to defend the faith but also to illuminate the inherent dignity of every human being, a foundational tenet of social justice. The convergence of these disciplines inspires a call to action, urging believers to uphold doctrinal integrity while vigorously pursuing justice in an unjust world, demonstrating the Church's unwavering dedication to both the defense of divine truth and the transformative power of love.

Common Theological Ground

Exploring the intricate dance between apologetics and social justice, one finds a shared stage in the Catholic conviction of defending faith and compassionately uplifting the marginalized. The "Option for the Poor and Vulnerable" urges a proactive lift of those trod down by inequity, akin to the advocacy for Christ's divinity that penetrates the layers of scripture and tradition. Each demands a truth—one that resonates through doctrines of mercy and incarnational love. This interconnectedness sees the divine in the plight of the poor, challenging apologetics to embrace a holistic view where social justice is not merely an adjunct but a tangible testament to Christ's living presence among us. Rooted in the belief that truth must walk hand in hand with charity, these theological pillars unite, affirming that justice for the marginalized is as divine a calling as the proclamation of Christ's lordship. Both streams converge into a singular creed of faith in action, inviting the Catholic Church to see the face of Christ in every act of justice pursued.

Doctrinal Connections The fascinating intersection where Catholic social justice meets Christian apologetics is like discovering a bridge joining two grand cathedrals of thought: one devoted to the temporal stewardship over earthly concerns, the other defending the eternal mysteries of divine revelation. This synthesis isn't merely theoretical; it's deeply doctrinal, giving substance to both communities through shared beliefs and values.

Both Catholic social justice and apologetic tradition root themselves firmly in doctrine central to the faith, particularly in matters concerning the respect and dignity of every person, created in the image of God. Social justice, epitomized by the "Option for the Poor and Vulnerable," translates this into a call for action—a demand that we prioritize the needs of the impoverished and marginalized, much as Jesus advocated during His earthly ministry.

The doctrine underscoring the divinity of Jesus isn't merely a theological assertion but a profound reality impacting moral and ethical imperatives. In recognizing Christ as divine, apologetics argues not just for His celestial authority but also for the divine imperative to love and serve the most vulnerable. This shared conceptual groundwork is both a natural and supernatural unity, an echo from heaven rebounding through earthly corridors.

The doctrinal essence of Jesus' dual nature—both divine and human—provides a rich vein of connection between apologetic defense and social justice. As the councils have defined, this divine humanity guides the faithful towards a form of justice that transcends human wisdom. His incarnational mission ties seamlessly with Catholic social teaching, revealing that our earthly acts of justice are fundamentally acts of honoring the divine image within humanity.

Through the lens of apologetic tradition, the divinity of Christ becomes not only a point defended by creed but a transformational truth compelling believers toward justice. Here lies an allegory of sorts: Christ as both just Judge and merciful Savior, a paradox that beckons Catholics to a higher calling. This connects to the heart of Catholic social justice, which extends beyond systemic critique to a profound empathy—a reflection of Christ's own ministry.

Moreover, justice in the context of divine truth is not a relative measure but a doctrinal one, grounded in the moral truths revealed by Christ Himself. This convergence emphasizes that earthly justice and divine justice are inseparable under the same doctrine, both flowing from the same wellspring of Holy Scripture and tradition. The truth affirmed in councils, and the teachings preserved by theologians across the ages, form a compelling unity between these realms.

Reflections on the development of doctrine reveal that each component of belief is interconnected. When we engage with the divinity of Christ, we're simultaneously called to engage with His world through justice. This isn't just an obligation but a profound invitation to participate in the divine drama where faith and action merge seamlessly, echoing the harmony intended by God for His creation.

The theological confluence found here is akin to a symphony—a beautifully orchestrated composition wherein apologetic acclaims and social advocacy echo with harmonious intent. They are notes written within the same divine score, engaging hearts and minds in a testament of faith that challenges the believer to recognize Christ in everyone, especially the poor and oppressed.

This is the doctrinal backbone binding these two expressions of faith: a creedal confession of Christ's divinity, recognized by councils and Church Fathers alike, carrying within it the ethical implications of social doctrine that guides us on every treacherous path of the temporal world. It impels a praxis that doesn't merely argue for truth but lives it.

As this bridge between apologetics and social justice rests on doctrinal connections, it provides a sturdy crossing. It leads us from intellectual assent to practical engagement, where every defense of divine truth is also a declaration of human dignity. Empowered by the Holy Spirit, the Church's mission gains coherence and strength.

In the end, these doctrinal ties serve as reminders that our faith is not a static relic but a living tradition, one that calls us to integrate belief with action. Herein lies the beauty of Catholic doctrine—in its ability to bind heaven to earth, belief to action, through the person of Jesus Christ, whose divine legacy moves both our hearts and our hands.

Practical Implications for Advocacy

In orchestrating a divine symphony of faith and action, the harmonious convergence of apologetics and social justice reveals itself as both an art and imperative. Advocacy finds its transformative power when the truth of Christ's divinity intertwines with our commitment to the marginalized. This union obligates believers to not merely defend doctrinal truths but to embody them in acts of justice. Where Christ's teachings shine through, the poor and vulnerable often stand illuminated at the center; thus, advocacy becomes a canvas where theological veracity meets tangible compassion. This profound alliance of divine understanding and social responsibility invites us to champion a world where the defense of faith is inseparable from the love of neighbor, echoing the very heart of Catholic doctrine. The challenge lies in crafting an advocacy that transcends mere words, urging us to continually translate sacred tenets into secular actions, thus venerating the same divinity we so ardently defend.

Strategies for Action Within the vast tapestry of Catholic doctrine, the threads of apologetics and social justice intertwine seamlessly, each reinforcing the other in the quest for spiritual and social renewal. The critical underpinning of this relationship is the belief that the proclamation of Christ's divinity need not be in opposition to the church's mission to uplift the poor and vulnerable. Instead, it offers a profound lens through which advocacy can be reframed, invigorated, and redirected towards action.

Action, as the harmonious blend of contemplation and commitment, stems from understanding that any act of justice is inherently tied to the acknowledgment of divine truths. The strategies devised herein, therefore, are not mere prescriptions for change but are indicative of a larger movement towards a more holistically Christian response to social ills.

Turning towards historical paradigms, we find that the early Church Fathers laid the groundwork in blending doctrine with duty. They didn't see the dissemination of theological truths and the act of serving the marginalized as mutually exclusive. Rather, each became the other's raison d'être. The method to revitalize this ethos today involves rekindling this historical synergy; thus, adopting a dual focus becomes imperative.

First, advocacy must be predicated on *integrative teaching sessions*. There's power in education, where apologetics serves not as a counter-argument to skepticism but as a platform to elevate community consciousness about social justice. Innovative platforms, whether in parishes or academic settings, must emphasize the unbreakable bond between divine justice as enshrined in Christ and the social demands it impels. These educational initiatives are best suited to not just inform but transform. They should be structured to inspire individuals to see every interaction with the marginalized as a direct contact with the Christological mystery.

A second, and potentially more challenging strategy is the facilitation of *open communal dialogues* wherein the ones most affected by poverty have a voice and place at the table— where they are not subjects of theological discourse but active participants in the conversation. Advocacy efforts must make room for the voices of the poor, framed not as charity cases but as bearers of divine wisdom. This shift in narrative invites a re-evaluation of how the divine is recognized amid human suffering.

Additionally, *partnerships with other faith and secular organizations* are essential to exceed the isolated effectiveness of a single-minded approach. Imagine a world where Catholic advocacy groups collaborate closely with non-Catholic entities, driven by a shared vision of justice anchored in love. These partnerships must respect doctrinal differences while not allowing those differences to overshadow the collective mission for social betterment.

Another approach is the creation of *apologetic-infused service projects* which marry verbal proclamation of faith with tangible acts of mercy. By weaving apologetic narratives into service activities, communities can witness the faith enacted as much as expounded. A soup kitchen can transform into a living testament of Christ's kingdom if accompanied by testimonies about the theological importance of service, shared in mutual celebration of the dignity of all recipients.

Furthermore, an imperative strategy for action involves the fearless use of modern technology for advocacy. Today's digital tools should be mastered not just for communication but also as venues for virtual apologetic dialogues coupled with justice-led campaigns. Social media and online platforms ought to amplify the teachings of Jesus, while simultaneously galvanizing support and mobilization for social causes. Here, the voices of the Church Fathers speak through pixels and bytes, as relevant now as centuries ago.

Lastly, *direct political engagement* cannot be underestimated as a potent strategy. Informed by Pope Leo XIII's encyclicals and the evolving social encyclical tradition, the faithful are called not just to pray but to politick—to lobby for laws that reflect divinely inspired justice. While navigating this terrain where church and state often find themselves at odds, the guiding principle remains the same: any policy to aid the least among us should be seen as an extension of Christological apologetics.

These strategies represent an amalgamation of theology and practice, aiming to weave apologetics and advocacy into a seamless garment of Christian witness. Through each strategy, a singular truth emerges: that the divine mandate to proclaim Christ cannot be disentangled from the call to love, uplift, and dignify every human being. Therefore, through education, dialogue, partnership, action, technology, and politics, the Catholic imperative to option for the poor becomes not just a theoretical concept but a lived reality.

In summation, these strategies offer roadmaps for the faithful eager to embody the gospel fully through action. Bridging apologetics with advocacy frames the mission of the Church not as disparate threads but as a coherent tapestry, vibrant and alive—a testament to the commitment that recognizing Christ's divinity is intertwined inexorably with meeting the needs of the poor.

Chapter 11: Case Studies and Applications

Turning our gaze toward the rich tapestry of history and its living threads in the modern world, we find profound lessons etched in the fabric of Catholic Social Justice and Apologetic thought. These case studies stand as testaments to the dynamic interplay between faith and action, urging us to reflect on the remarkable congruence between advocating for the impoverished and affirming the divine nature of Christ. Through historical narratives, we discern how past endeavors have shaped present understandings, teaching us that true advocacy is not merely an act of charity but a manifestation of the divine mandate. Meanwhile, contemporary applications remind us that the principles illuminating the option for the vulnerable and the apologetic for Christ's divinity are alive, calling us to realms both metaphysical and practical. The intertwining of these paths urges a holistic engagement with theology—a commitment to live and breathe doctrine in ways that transform not just the mind and soul but societies and systems. Thus, as we analyze these cases, our challenge is to distill these principles into practices that resonate and reverberate across time, echoing the dual imperatives of justice and faith.

Historical Case Studies

Delving into the annals of history, we encounter a tapestry woven with both the gold threads of divine advocacy and the humble fibers of earthly justice. Consider the profound legacy of St. Francis of Assisi, whose radical embrace of poverty arguably exemplifies the divine paradox: losing oneself to find a richer spiritual inheritance. His life serves as both testament and apologetic, a living argument for Christ's divinity embodied through radical openness to the other. Then, we observe the actions of Bartolomé de las Casas, whose defense of indigenous peoples in the New World stands as an early beacon of social justice rooted in Christian theology. Las Casas' efforts were not mere humanist endeavors; they were deeply theological, resting on a Christocentric claim—that all are made in the image of God and deserve dignity. These case studies serve as allegories, where the social and the sacred dance, not as disparate partners but as a unified force, compelling us to reinterpret justice through a divine lens, each step echoing Christ's call to love and protect the vulnerable.

Lessons Learned The tapestry of history is a teacher unlike any other, and when we examine the historical case studies through the lens of Catholic doctrine, particular lessons emerge with clarity. Viewing the past through the principles of Catholic Social Justice and the divine apologetics of Jesus illuminates the dichotomy between temporal power and spiritual integrity. One lesson learned from these historical cases is that the Church's advocacy for the poor and vulnerable is not merely a response to social conditions but is deeply rooted in the theological belief that divinity itself found expression among the destitute and disenfranchised.

History reveals that the Church has often walked a precarious path between earthly authority and heavenly mandates. This delicate balance underscores a critical lesson: the upholding of social justice within Catholic theology serves not only as an ethical demand but as a spiritual necessity. Instances where the Church has aligned itself too closely with political powers often resulted in compromises that undermined its intrinsic mission of advocating for the poor and revealing the face of Christ in the suffering.

The engagement with historical contexts allows us to trace a continuity of mission from the early Christian community to modern times. In the face of persecution, early Christians learned that their strength lay not in political power but in a radical commitment to the Gospel's message of love and justice. This principle holds true through various historical epochs, such as in the lives of Saint Francis of Assisi and Saint Vincent de Paul, who embodied the Church's call to "Option for the Poor" by living among, serving, and uplifting the marginalized.

One poignant lesson from these case studies is the Church's role as both prophet and servant. As prophet, it must speak truth to power, challenging structures that perpetuate inequality and injustice. As servant, it must fulfill its vocation by offering tangible aid and hope to those in need. This dual role requires discernment and courage, as seen in the actions of many church leaders and laity who have responded to the cries of the poor with both charity and advocacy, sometimes at great personal cost.

The historical narratives also teach us about the power of communal belief. When the Church has empowered its members to act collectively for justice, the results have often been transformative. Movements inspired by Catholic teaching—such as the Catholic Worker Movement—illustrate how communal action rooted in faith can challenge societal norms and bring about significant social change. This echoes the apologetic view that faith, when practiced authentically, becomes a witness to the divine truths it seeks to proclaim.

Moreover, historical case studies remind us of the tension between tradition and progress within the Church itself. Balancing the wealth of theological heritage with the demands of contemporary social issues requires an openness to the Spirit's guidance, ensuring that traditions remain vibrant and relevant. The lessons of history caution against the rigidity that can arise from an overly dogmatic interpretation of doctrine, urging instead for a dynamic and compassionate application that resonates with the changing circumstances of human lives.

Crucially, these studies reveal that understanding and addressing poverty is not just an economic or social endeavor but is deeply intertwined with recognizing the inherent dignity of every person as part of the divine creation. This realization shifts the focus from mere problem-solving to fostering relationships that reflect the compassion and justice of God. It is this recognition that stands as a testament to the intrinsic connection between Catholic Social Justice and the apologetic defense of Jesus' divinity.

Ultimately, historical insights shed light on the enduring question of how the Church can maintain its prophetic voice without compromising its foundational beliefs. The cases studied reveal a paradox: true power and authority in the Christian sense are found in humility, service, and love. In this respect, the historical path of the Church serves as both a mirror and a map for navigating contemporary challenges, constantly guiding us back to the core of Christ's teachings.

In summary, the lessons learned from historical case studies challenge us to approach the future with both humility and boldness. They urge us to consider how we can continue to forge paths of justice, love, and truth in our contemporary world, learning from past missteps and building upon successes. As we reflect on these lessons, they remind us that the Church's mission is perennial, adapting to new contexts while remaining steadfast in its commitment to embodying the love and justice of Christ among all people, especially the poor and vulnerable.

Modern Applications

Venture into the tapestry of modernity, where the ancient threads of Catholic Social Justice and Apologetics for the divinity of Jesus Christ intertwine with contemporary fabrics, crafting a garment fit for the today's societal canvas. Here, the age-old tenet of preferential care for the poor and vulnerable does not merely echo in ecclesiastical corridors or linger in theological treatises; it manifests tangibly in the urban landscapes characterized by disparity and in the digital ether pulsating with discourse. The dialogical engagement between faith and action morphs into vibrant programs that leverage technology to advocate for dignity, embody stewardship, and execute mercy. Within this context, apologetic fervor dynamically defends the divinity of Christ not just at pulpits but online, where skepticism abounds, requiring believers to wield both faith and reason harmoniously. The convergence of these two strands—care and creed—alongside sociological insights, becomes a modern panoply for addressing the wounds and wonders of our shared human experience. This synthesis, much like an allegorical dance, is ever-evolving, shaping and reshaping as it maneuvers through the ebb and flow of time's relentless march.

Contemporary Examples detail the living testament of Catholic social justice's alchemy when merged seamlessly with apologetics, creating a modern mosaic reflective of first-century foundations. In our rapidly shifting world, where the tides of socio-cultural norms advance with unprecedented haste, the essence of the "Option for the Poor and Vulnerable" pulses with renewed vitality, finding expression in varied and vivid arenas.

The poignant narrative of Catholic charities stands as a beacon among contemporary examples, signifying the Church's enduring commitment to Christ's call toward those marginalized and impoverished. Organizations like the Catholic Relief Services not only respond to humanitarian crises with tangible aid but do so guided by doctrines that emphasize empathy and dignity. Their work exemplifies a living apologetics—demonstrating the harmony between the divine mission of Jesus and the social mandate to uplift the downtrodden.

In communities across continents, new Catholic movements have arisen, adeptly marrying the theological with the practical. Consider the rise of ethical banking initiatives such as those championed by the Vatican. These efforts aim not just at ethical financial practices but reveal an apologetic dialog intertwined with economic justice. By committing to financial inclusivity and transparency, these institutions embody a modern reinterpretation of parables where the meek and humble disrupt traditional power structures.

There are also compelling examples within educational spheres. As Catholic schools and universities embrace broader curricula that integrate social justice as core, they champion a holistic educating that bridges theological discourse and academic inquiry. The incorporation of service-learning programs where students engage directly with underserved communities underscores the union of theology and action. This pedagogical approach does more than impart knowledge; it breathes life into apologetics by compelling students to wrestle with the divine in the midst of human struggle.

Amid this landscape of applied theology, the rise of lay movements cannot be ignored. Groups like the Focolare and Sant'Egidio actively engage in social advocacy while deeply rooted in spiritual contemplation. Their efforts illustrate the Church's teaching on the preferential option for the poor through community upliftment, while simultaneously delving into the Christological mystery—expressing doctrine through the art of lived witness.

Meanwhile, the application of Catholic tenets in the digital realm emerges as a new frontier. Online ministries and platforms offer a synthesizing of ancient truths with cutting-edge technology, reaching a generation that lives both online and offline. Here, where dialogues about social justice intersect with questions on the identity of Christ, digital outreach offers a contemporary apologetic engagement where theology embraces technology in service of truth and mercy.

The ecological movement within the Church also provides a contemporary lens through which we view Catholic doctrine in action. The encyclical "Laudato Si'" catalyzed not only the Church but broader society toward ecological justice. This movement's influence reaches across borders, advocating for a planetary option for the vulnerable—both human and non-human. Such expressions renew our comprehension of interconnectedness, echoing the harmony of Christ with creation, thus breathing new life into apologetic discourses that defend and articulate the divine through care for our common home.

Inextricably linked to these expressions is the dynamic role of Catholic healthcare institutions globally. They serve as bastions of Christ's healing ministry, particularly in regions lacking in medical resources. Hospitals and clinics adhere to a compassionate ethos that resonates deeply with both social justice perspectives and apologetic affirmations of Christ as the ultimate healer. This harmonious confluence redefines the Church's narrative in contemporary society, where faith meets health in the service of profound dignity and enduring hope.

Such examples underscore that the intertwining of Catholic social doctrine with apologetics is no mere academic exercise; it's a lived, breathing reality. The Church's body, both mystical and organizational, manifests these truths through the earnest work of countless individuals and communities. Every act of advocacy, every gesture of mercy, becomes an inscription of divine logos into the substrate of human experience. Truly, this intricate tapestry of contemporary examples crafts a narrative where the ancient dances with the new, perpetually articulating the divine through the deeply human.

Chapter 12: Future Directions in Theology and Advocacy

As humanity stands at the cusp of unprecedented challenges and opportunities, it becomes imperative for theology and advocacy to explore new horizons. In this intricate tapestry of belief and action, theology must engage with emerging questions that extend beyond doctrinal confines to the heart of social justice, interweaving it seamlessly with the defense of faith. The evolving narrative of Catholic Social Teaching underscores the continual journey towards a just society where the dignity of every individual, especially the marginalized, stands affirmed not merely in word, but through compassionate and tangible action. Advocates, theologians, and scholars must collaborate, drawing from ancient wisdom while daring to innovate. This future beckons a reevaluation of the apology for Christ's divinity, not only as an intellectual exercise but as a living testament that radiates in acts of justice. Each new direction, then, becomes a path carved with the dual intent of deepening the faith and expanding its transformative power amidst global injustice, resonating with a truth that mercy and advocacy are inseparable partners on this pilgrim journey.

Emerging Theological Trends

In a world replete with rapid changes and unpredictable challenges, the landscape of theology is porous to innovations, reflecting an age characterized by cultural cross-pollination and existential quests for meaning. Emerging trends pivot around integrating deeper ecological awareness with age-old doctrines, merging the sanctity of life with the urgency for environmental sustainability. This interconnection hints at a theological renaissance where stewardship of creation reflects the ethos of protecting the poor and vulnerable, blurring the lines between cosmic and creaturely concerns. Additionally, there's a stronger emphasis on dialogical engagement with science and technology, striving for a symbiosis rather than antagonism, revealing a dynamic Catholic thought process that seeks truth as a comprehensive narrative. These trends showcase a robust advocacy for social justice that aligns seamlessly with a profound understanding of Jesus' divinity, inviting the faithful into a journey where the sacred and the social intertwine in life's canvas. The result is a theology enriched by tradition yet invigorated by contemporary calls to action, promising a vibrant future for those seeking to bridge faith with pragmatism.

Future Scholarship The horizon of theological inquiry unfurls before us, pregnant with possibilities as insistent as the dawn. As we navigate the confluence of Catholic Social Justice and Apologetics, the emerging theological trends beckon scholars to delve deeper into the heart of both disciplines. On the one hand, there's a nuanced interrogation of the divine narrative that shapes our understanding of Jesus. On the other, lies the fecund field of social justice, which demands the synthesis of doctrine with the lived realities of the marginalized.

The crossroads where theology and advocacy meet is not a static place but an ever-evolving landscape. Future scholarship must address questions as old as they are new, threading the needle between tradition and innovation. How can the immutable truths of Christ's divinity engage dynamically with the mutable conditions of human societies? How can the theological be a handmaiden to the practical in addressing poverty and marginalization? These questions are not merely academic; they are existential, requiring a rigorous dialogue between the ancients and the moderns.

A rich avenue for future exploration lies in the integration of neglected voices in theological discourse. Postcolonial and liberation theologies, for instance, offer perspectives that amplify the importance of the Option for the Poor. These voices can critically illuminate the intersection of power, culture, and belief, providing a broader canvas upon which to paint the reality of a gospel not just preached, but lived. How might these underexplored perspectives further the church's mission in a globalized world?

Moreover, there's the fascinating prospect of interdisciplinary approaches. Sociologists and anthropologists provide invaluable tools for understanding the cultural and systemic roots of poverty, which dogmatic theology alone might not sufficiently explain. Partnering these disciplines with theology fosters a robust framework capable of confronting modern exigencies with wisdom steeped in tradition yet agile enough for new challenges. Such collaboration could enrich apologetic discourse, especially in framing social justice issues as intrinsic to the understanding of Christ's mission on earth.

Then there's digital theology, an emerging frontier that holds promise for transformative effect. In an age where information disseminates at the speed of light, how can digital platforms be harnessed to advocate effectively for the poor, while simultaneously strengthening the apologetic framework for faith? This isn't merely about broadcasting; it's about building communities of faith that transcend geographical limitations. It's a call to witness, not just through catechesis but through visible acts of justice and love.

Future scholarship will also be tasked with addressing the pressing environmental crises and their theological implications. This 'green' theology can't be sequestered as a niche interest but must be integrated into the understanding of social justice. What does it mean to exercise the Option for the Poor in a world facing climate change? Are not the poor often the first to suffer from environmental degradation caused by the wealthy? Integrating ecological concerns within the theological framework offers a profound opportunity to embody stewardship in both earthly and spiritual realms.

Yet perhaps the most elusive, and thus most exciting, opportunity for future scholarship lies in the harmonization of historical theological insights with contemporary social mores. Here lies the challenge: staying true to the timeless tenets of faith while dynamically engaging with shifting cultural landscapes. How can theologians respect doctrinal integrity while being attuned to the complex, sometimes contradicting, currents of modern life? This requires a delicate balance and a willingness to engage with uncertainty, ambiguity, and even dissent.

Ultimately, future scholarly endeavors in the realm of theology and advocacy will need to maintain a dialogical rapport with the historical and cultural contexts that have shaped and continue to shape them. This dynamic interplay can provide not only insights for academic study but also practical strategies for real-world application. It's an invitation to rethink, reinterpret, and potentially revolutionize how the divine mystery is lived out in acts of justice and love.

In conclusion, the trajectory of future scholarship will pivot around questions that are both urgent and enduring. Through interdisciplinary collaboration, the inclusion of diverse voices, digital innovations, ecological consciousness, and historical grounding, the future holds boundless potential for advancing theological scholarship. Scholars taking these paths might find themselves not only uncovering deeper truths about the mysteries of faith but also contributing to a world more just and more aligned with the gospel's core imperatives.

The Role of Social Justice in Apologetics

In the ever-evolving landscape of theological inquiry and advocacy, the intersection of social justice and apologetics provides both a beacon and a challenge. At its core, Catholic Social Justice and apologetics for Jesus' divinity share a profound commonality in their pursuit of truth and moral imperative. By embracing the preferential option for the poor, adherents illuminate Christ's divinity, which embodies both profound empathy and divine transcendence. The teachings of Jesus invite us to recognize the marginalized as reflections of God's own image, thereby reinforcing the theological foundation of His divine nature. In a world riddled with complexities and inequities, the role of social justice in defending faith becomes not just an intellectual exercise but a living testament to the Gospel's power. This dynamic interplay invites theologians and advocates alike to forge pathways where conviction and compassion meet, emboldened by the knowledge that divine wisdom is inseparable from the love of neighbor. As such, social justice in apologetic discourse stands as a testament to the authenticity of faith, challenging us to see orthodoxy not as mere assent to doctrine but as an active journey towards justice and truth embodied in the earthly mission of Jesus Christ.

New Approaches In the grand symphony of theology and advocacy, the crescendo of new approaches in linking social justice and apologetics emerges like a melody that seeks to harmonize the dissonant notes of modernity with the timeless chords of divine truth. This emerging movement endeavors to weave social justice into the very fabric of apologetic discourse, situating the preferential option for the poor and vulnerable as a critical touchstone for defending the divinity of Christ. To embark on this journey is to acknowledge that the love for one's neighbor is not merely a moral adjunct but a hermeneutic lens through which the mystery of Christ can be better apprehended.

Apologetics, traditionally ensconced in rational discourse and philosophical argumentation, is undergoing a quiet metamorphosis. Consider the proposition that audaciously integrates the tenets of Catholic social justice into its very foundation. This evolution dares to ask: what if the credibility of the Christian claim about Jesus' divinity is best evidenced not solely through propositions and doctrines but also through the praxis of justice that mirrors His teachings? This approach thus extends beyond the textual and historical; it reaches for the transformative, asserting that a lived theology might reveal more about divine nature than syllogisms articulate.

Indeed, this pursuit involves an intricate dance with the paradox of grace and works, where the acts of love and mercy toward the least among us are seen as the most cogent testimony to the Incarnation. Apologists are called not only to deftly wield words but to live out the Gospel mandate in a world longing for signs of authentic hope. It becomes necessary, therefore, to craft a new apologetic narrative—one that intertwines theological sophistication with ethical imperatives woven into the daily existence of believers.

Historically, Catholic thinkers have often stood at the intersection of faith and reason—a tradition that invites fresh inquiry today. In imagining new approaches, the apologist might draw from this wellspring while simultaneously immersing themselves in the cries of the marginalized. This interplay of scholarly tradition with lived advocacy invites a reevaluation of apologetics' purpose, birthing a richer, more dynamic defense of faith. Here, the option for the poor becomes both a moral ethos and an existential declaration that Christ's divinity is inherently linked to His identification with the downtrodden.

Moreover, apologetics that embrace social justice inherently open themselves to the global contexts of suffering and inequity. This perspective not only enriches the internal dialogue within the Church but also extends an invitation to the secular and interfaith communities, fostering a shared pursuit of justice. In doing so, it resituates the Church's apologetic endeavor as a collaborative mission to uphold human dignity, one that finds its genesis in the divine love manifest in Christ—a love that requires no defense beyond the visible testament of charity.

This approach also provides a counter-narrative to the critiques of irrelevance that often challenge religious institutions today. By embedding the principles of social justice within apologetic missions, the Church rejuvenates its voice, making it resonate more effectively with a generation yearning for authenticity and tangible compassion. With these newfound methodologies, Catholic apologetics is poised not to recede into an ivory tower but to reach into the public square, armed with an ethic of care as its greatest apologetic weapon.

Furthermore, integrating social justice into apologetics demands an ongoing, dynamic dialogue between theological doctrines and contemporary realities. As apologists engage with this emerging paradigm, they must cultivate humility and openness. The willingness to learn from social sciences, philosophy, and other disciplines enriches the discourse. By situating Jesus' divinity within the broader tapestry of human experience and struggle, apologists offer a nuanced, relevant, and compelling case for faith that speaks directly to the human heart's deepest longings.

Additionally, this is not just an intellectual exercise; it is a call to action. Theoretical frameworks must inspire concrete commitments to justice work and advocacy endeavors, which are integral to this newfound apologetic ethos. Whether through community service, public policy engagement, or global partnerships aimed at alleviating poverty and injustice, these actions become the most eloquent defense of the divine claim that love indeed transforms the world.

Practically, these new approaches could involve reimagining catechetical programs and theological education to foreground social justice alongside traditional apologetic topics. Workshops, seminars, and dialogues centered on Jesus' teachings and His direct involvement with society's marginalized can inspire both young and seasoned believers to embody this blended mission of faith and justice. Moreover, such initiatives invite an inculturated theology that respects and responds to the distinct cultural and societal contexts in which faith communities are situated.

Indeed, to envision a future where apologetics and social justice converge is to stand shoulder to shoulder with the Church's prophetic tradition. Part of reimagining new approaches involves reviving the Church's historical commitment to the marginalized as a form of testimony that echoes the early disciples' fervor. Apologists today, much like their ancestral counterparts, are tasked with articulating a vision of the kingdom that is less a matter of talk and more an embodiment of transformative love.

Ultimately, these new approaches issue a profound invitation to believers and skeptics alike to view faith not merely as a series of doctrinal claims but as a vibrant, ongoing narrative of love and justice unfolding in the world. As this approach continues to evolve, it ensures that apologetics will remain a vital force, one that invites all people into a communal journey of understanding the divine found in acts of grace and mercy.

Conclusion

The journey we've traveled through the complex interconnections of Catholic Social Justice and Apologetics for the divinity of Jesus Christ leads us now to a vantage point, from which we can appreciate the tapestry woven from these threads. As we conclude, the notion of intertwining faith with social action emerges as both a historical constant and a future imperative.

At the heart of Catholic teaching lies a profound option for the poor and vulnerable—a principle that illuminates the divine in the human condition. This unyielding focus on the marginalized reflects not just a charitable sentiment, but a theological assertion. It's a stark acknowledgment that severs the superficial from the substantial in religious life. When Catholicism opts for the poor, it fundamentally asserts that justice isn't a tertiary doctrine but a core demand of the Gospel.

In tandem, the apologetic enterprise seeks not only to defend but to define. Defending the divinity of Jesus Christ isn't a mere academic exercise. It's a declaration of the paradox of transcendence and imminence: God in the human form, subject to poverty, affliction, and sacrifice. Apologetics reinforces this mystery, providing a rationale for the otherwise enigmatic truth of a God who walks with the destitute.

What then binds social justice and apologetics is not just shared theology, but a shared mission—a symphony where doctrine harmonizes with deeds, and belief engenders action. This binding isn't merely institutional but is the evocative relational bond of faith and practice.

The teachings of Christ, encapsulated in the Gospels, serve as a dual beacon. They urge believers to embrace the marginalized in radical solidarity and simultaneously proclaim His divine nature. Through the narratives of Jesus' life, His engagement with the outcasts becomes both an apologetic artifact and a social manifesto.

Additionally, the Church Fathers provide a timeless dialogue on these themes. Their writings elucidate an unwavering commitment to justice that is germane not just to their era, but resonates through centuries. They elevate a faith that isn't idle but alive—a faith that transforms societies by uplifting the least among their members.

In considering papal encyclicals and council pronouncements, we witness historical epochs where church authority resonates with moral urgency. The institutional church steps into temporal realms with a confidence that is both prophetic and pastoral. These documents, addressing social injustices, interlace theological tenets with practical exhortations for reform and renewal.

Yet, moving forward, the dialogue doesn't end with historical reflections. Contemporary issues like global poverty, ecological degradation, and systemic injustice demand a new vigor. This era beckons theologians and social advocates to synergize theory and praxis. The Church's response must be both profound in thought and pragmatic in application.

The linkage between apologetics and social justice forms a compelling narrative that requires continuous evolution. It's an evolving hermeneutic that calls for rigorous scholarship alongside impassioned activism. As doctrine and action continue to integrate, their resultant synergy offers the potential for genuine transformation—not just within the Church, but throughout the global society.

This conclusion does not serve as a final word but as a call to action. To uphold the divinity of Christ in word demands that it be upheld in deed. True apologetics will be recognized not solely by eloquent argument but by living testimony of justice enacted. As followers of a faith built upon the teachings and example of a Savior who embraced the outcasts, believers are called to emulate this divine model in relentless pursuit of social justice.

May this journey through Catholic Social Justice and Apologetics inspire renewed commitment and fresh insights. It's a reminder that the Church exists not only to preach but to practice, not merely to defend dogmas but to demonstrate them through committed love and justice for all, especially the poor and vulnerable. As these principles are lived out with integrity, the world will increasingly catch glimpses of the divine, alive and active, ever among us.

Appendix A: Appendix

In the heart of the Church's vast and intricate tapestry lies a profound intertwining of doctrine and discourse, woven with the threads of tradition and revelation. This appendix seeks to illuminate the needlepoint where the Catholic Church's enduring commitment to the Option for the Poor and Vulnerable intersects with the apologetic fervor defending the divinity of Jesus Christ. From the orations of the Church Fathers to the deliberations of ecumenical councils, a harmonious dialogue emerges, uniting the moral and the metaphysical. The social imperatives invoked by Catholics echo the divine rhetoric of Christ's mission—a mission manifest in bringing justice to the marginalized and asserting His divine identity. In combing through relevant papal documents and major councils, one encounters a symphony of guiding wisdom that not only champions social doctrine but also embodies the sacred narrative of Christ as divine liberator. Indeed, herein lies a testament to a Church that stands unwavering at the confluence of spiritual conviction and social conscience.

Key Papal Documents Relevant to Social Justice

The annals of papal writings offer a rich tapestry through which one can trace the evolution of Catholic social teaching, particularly on the issue of social justice. These documents articulate the Church's enduring concern for the plight of the marginalized and establish a theological framework that underscores its commitment to the option for the poor and vulnerable. As these documents unfold through history, they weave a narrative of advocacy, marrying the esoteric depths of theological reflection with the palpable needs of the world.

Rerum Novarum, the seminal encyclical promulgated by Pope Leo XIII in 1891, stands as a cornerstone of modern Catholic social thought. It responded to the challenges of industrialization, addressing the rights and duties of labor and capital. By emphasizing the dignity of workers and the necessity of just wages, Leo XIII's document was a clarion call for the Church to engage actively in economic discourse. Indeed, it marked the Church's first major foray into the social questions of the modern era—an era characterized by profound economic disparities and class conflict.

Following in this tradition, *Quadragesimo Anno*, written by Pope Pius XI in 1931, came at a time of global economic turmoil. Building upon the principles of *Rerum Novarum*, it expanded the Church's concerns to include systemic injustices within the economic order. Pius XI introduced the notion of subsidiarity, advocating for social structures that empower smaller communities rather than over-centralizing power and resources. The encyclical painted a vivid picture of a world in need of equity and collaboration, emphasizing the moral dimensions of economic activity.

Pope John XXIII's *Mater et Magistra* and *Pacem in Terris* released during the early 1960s, furthered this development, emphasizing human dignity and global solidarity. With world peace hanging by a thread during the Cold War, *Pacem in Terris* called for international dialogue and disarmament, underscoring the belief that true peace must be built on justice and charity. These documents prophetically outlined a vision of the world defined by interconnectedness and mutual respect, transcending borders and ideologies.

The Second Vatican Council (1962-1965) was another watershed moment, greatly influencing subsequent papal writings on social justice. *Gaudium et Spes*, one of the Council's most significant documents, lamented the dichotomy between the rich and the poor as an affront to humanity and proposed a model of the Church that walks in the world with a deep sensitivity to social dynamics. This represented an ecclesiological shift whereby the Church declared its intent to be a beacon of hope amid temporal trials.

Intriguingly, Pope Paul VI's *Populorum Progressio* in 1967 extended these concerns to the realities of global development. It painted a harrowing picture of inequality and called for development to be a new name for peace. This encyclical urged richer nations to aid poorer ones, highlighting economic interdependence and prioritizing integral human development. Paul VI's vision was inclusive, calling for a world where the economic pie grows rather than only its distribution changing.

Pope John Paul II's contributions to the discourse through documents such as *Laborem Exercens* (1981), *Sollicitudo Rei Socialis* (1987), and *Centesimus Annus* (1991), brought the teachings alive with his philosophical insights and global perspective. He resisted both blind capitalism and collectivist socialism, advocating instead for a society where economic systems serve human freedom and dignity. His encyclicals elucidated the inherent connections between work, the economy, and the moral order.

One cannot ignore *Evangelii Gaudium*, released by Pope Francis, which critiques a world economy driven by "an economy of exclusion and inequality". In this apostolic exhortation, Francis speaks candidly against the idolatry of money and calls the Catholic community to reassess values and ensure they are aligned with the Gospel's call to a preferential option for the poor. His words resonate as a call to action, urging all people of goodwill to construct a world marked by justice and compassion.

Furthermore, *Laudato Si'*, also by Pope Francis, represents an environmental dimension to the Church's social doctrine. By addressing ecological degradation, he underscores the intimate link between environmental stewardship and social justice, urging the faithful to care for our common home as a responsibility that corresponds to caring for the marginalized. This document challenges the Church globally to recognize how societal ills and environmental issues are interwoven.

This corpus of papal writings, while diverse in its individual emphasis, collectively underscores a fundamental theme: human dignity is the spine that supports the Church's social magisterium. As a compass, these documents guide not only Catholics but all humanity toward an ethos where justice, peace, and solidarity reign supreme. They invite theologians, social scientists, and lay faithful alike to engage the world with a heart and mind molded by these teachings, striving for a civitas dei—a city of God where love and justice prevail as tangible realities.

By anchoring its approach in such theological and philosophical profundities, the Church crafts a narrative that is not merely responsive to ephemeral challenges but is rooted in eternal truths that transcend temporal limitations. These papal documents forge a path in the moral wilderness, inviting humanity to transcend its plight and embrace the divine call to justice and love, beckoning each person to live, not merely for oneself, but in solidarity with others.

In bitter and sweet times alike, when society grapples with ethical dilemmas and systemic injustices, these foundational documents serve as a reservoir of wisdom and hope. They light the way, reminding the faithful that the pursuit of social justice is not an optional endeavor but a central tenet of living out the Gospel. Such words shine brightly, urging the Church to be an instrument of peace and an advocate for the poor, never ceasing to echo the call that arches heavenward, compelling a response to the cries of the downtrodden.

Major Councils and Their Declarations on Social Issues

In the grand tapestry of Catholic tradition, ecumenical councils have played pivotal roles, like illustrious scenes, unveiling pivotal declarations that impact social doctrines. Their deliberations go beyond abstract theological discourse, marking indelible ink on the annals of history through their determined attention to social issues. These councils, responding to the winds of change, had to balance between the immutable doctrines of faith and the mutable needs of society.

The Council of Nicaea in 325 AD, perhaps best known for its dogmatic clarifications, set an early precedent that social issues and doctrine are not mutually exclusive. Although its main focus was the clarification of Christ's divinity, the council indirectly established a template for how the Church might think about hierarchical structures, power dynamics, and communal responsibilities, which are all inherently social in nature.

Fast forward to the Middle Ages, the Fourth Lateran Council of 1215 issued comprehensive canons not only to address heresies but also socio-political structures, articulating a nascent form of social consensus that looked beyond the throne. It condemned abuses such as usury and called for the fair treatment of individuals within the societal frameworks of the time. This coupling of faith and concern for justice was to echo throughout the centuries, serving as a clarion call for social reform linked intricately with the Gospel's radical option for the oppressed.

The Council of Trent in the 16th century, navigating the treacherous waters of the Reformation, also grappled with issues that transcended pure dogma. While its directives on the sacraments stood out, Trent indirectly broached social justice by reaffirming the Church's authority to correct moral abuses and uphold its spiritual mandates. Drinking deeply from the well of scriptural wisdom, Trent subtly reinforced a justice-centered view that leadership entails the service of all, especially the marginalized.

The 19th and early 20th centuries marked a new philosophical era and with it came transformative councils that could no longer ignore the pressing social quandaries of a modernizing world. Vatican I convened during a period of burgeoning industrialization and its ensuing societal inequalities. Its major work, however, was cut short by external political upheavals, leaving the Church yearning for a comprehensive engagement with emerging social doctrines. Yet its short-lived momentum set the stage for its successor council.

Vatican II, convened in the 1960s, revolutionized the Church's social doctrine. The council's documents, particularly *Gaudium et Spes*, carved out a new path for the Church to actively engage with the world's social issues. It was at this landmark council that the principle of social justice found a robust, articulate champion. The bishops called upon all Catholics to see the face of Christ in the poor and to work collectively towards a society that embraced the inherent dignity of each person.

In focusing on the Church's relationship with the modern world, Vatican II provided a roadmap that linked ecclesial mission with social advocacy. It unequivocally affirmed that Catholic doctrine is not only about the sacred mysteries of faith but also about transforming the world's social order into one of compassion, equity, and solidarity. Here, the council magnanimously unfolded its armory of declarations aiming to illuminate the moral and social challenges that had clamored for attention from the folds of history.

Subsequent councils and synods have continued to reiterate and build upon the foundations laid by Vatican II. The teachings that flowed from these gatherings continued to march toward justice like an unyielding river, mindful of the turbulence of the secular world. They persist to this day to articulate a vision where tradition informs action and faith mandates justice.

This exploration of major councils reminds us that the Church's response to social issues has been not just reactive but deeply proactive. The conciliar process gave birth to a rich lineage of social teachings that challenge each generation to forge a link between eternal truths and temporal needs. In these councils, the echoes of divine justice continue to reverberate, heralding the Church's unending agon over injustice and inequity.

It is through these panels of wisdom that councils have imbued Catholics with the theological rigor needed to battle against the spectre of injustice. These monumental gatherings of the faithful underscore a profound message that theological reflection finds its fulfillment in justice, mirroring the divine law. Their declarations, though emanating from ancient times, remain ever pertinent, calling us to a deeper understanding and enactment of social justice.

Annotated Bibliography for Further Reading

In the labyrinth of thought where faith and reason intertwine, this annotated bibliography offers a curated pathway through the tapestry of Catholic social justice and apologetics. Each selected work invites the reader to ponder the dimensions where theology meets advocacy, and dogma dances with human dignity.

The Compendium of the Social Doctrine of the Church edited by the Pontifical Council for Justice and Peace is an essential foundation. This text systematically presents the Church's teachings on social matters, allowing readers to appreciate the intricate balance between pastoral care and intellectual rigor. It provides a comprehensive overview of the principles underpinning Catholic social justice, with particular emphasis on the Option for the Poor.

Gustavo Gutierrez's *A Theology of Liberation*, an enigmatic masterpiece, boldly introduces liberation theology, urging a rethinking of how poverty and faith interrelate. His work is both a theological and philosophical exploration that ignites critical reflection. Gutierrez makes an impassioned call for a preferential option for the poor, a resonant echo in the corridors of ecclesial thought.

For a deeper understanding of Pauline theology and its socio-political dimensions, *The Politics of Paul: The Political Implications of Pauline Theology* by Neil Elliott presents a compelling exegesis. Elliott dissects the apostle's letters through a contemporary lens, highlighting themes that advocate for justice and equality. His discourse is invaluable for those exploring the nexus of scripture and modern social justice.

Turning to apologetics, *The Resurrection of the Son of God* by N.T. Wright stands as a monumental contribution. Wright systematically defends the historical and theological claims of Jesus' resurrection. It's an analytical triumph that underpins many apologetic arguments, grounding them in historical context and theological profundity. His erudition sheds light on the role of Christ's divinity in the symphony of salvation history.

The classic work of C.S. Lewis, *Mere Christianity*, cannot be overlooked. Though not explicitly Catholic, Lewis's cogent case for Christian doctrine provides a robust foundation for understanding the rational underpinnings of faith. His logic appeals across denominational lines, offering insights that are both fundamental and eloquent.

David Bentley Hart's *The Beauty of the Infinite: The Aesthetics of Christian Truth* explores the intersection of aesthetics, metaphysics, and theology. Hart provocatively suggests how beauty itself is a path to divine truth, a notion significantly tied to the incarnation and divinity of Christ. His intricate prose challenges readers to consider the apologetic importance of beauty in revealing God.

On the ground where practice meets theory, John A. Coleman's *Globalization and Catholic Social Thought* examines the Catholic Church's response to globalization. Coleman provides a critical view on how the Church's social teachings adapt to modern challenges, rooting these responses in both tradition and innovation. His exploration of global interconnectedness complements discussions about the social impact of Catholic doctrine.

In addressing Church tradition and its development, Yves Congar's *True and False Reform in the Church* is seminal. Congar navigates ecclesial reform and the perpetual balancing act of maintaining fidelity to tradition while embracing necessary change. His insights are invaluable for comprehending how social justice teachings develop in fidelity with Church doctrine.

Philip Yancey's *The Jesus I Never Knew* engages with the enigmatic figure of Jesus, weaving together a portrait that is both personal and theological. Yancey's approach illuminates Christ's humanity and divinity, sparking reflections on how these dual natures underpin the Church's social mission. His narrative is a catalyst for deeper engagement with Christological doctrines.

Theology for a Troubled Believer: An Introduction to the Christian Faith by Diogenes Allen presents theology in an accessible manner, arguing that true Christian belief must grapple with suffering and doubt. Allen's reflections provide fertile ground for discussions on social justice and divine compassion, offering readers a framework for integrating doubts into a cohesive faith journey.

Henri Nouwen's *Rich in Spirit* explores the paradox of spiritual poverty and wealth, a pivotal concept in Catholic spirituality that mirrors social justice's concerns. Nouwen's narrative highlights the interior journey essential for authentic Christian living, emphasizing how spiritual richness equips believers to advocate for the materially poor.

Joseph Ratzinger (Pope Benedict XVI) offers a profound theological meditation in his *Introduction to Christianity*. Ratzinger delves into the complexities of faith, exploring the existential undercurrents that affirm Christ's divinity and the implications for contemporary believers. His synthesis of Catholic doctrine provides a robust defense of the faith against modern skepticism.

Christus Vivit (Christ Lives) by Pope Francis speaks with a pastoral heart to the youth of the world, but its implications for social justice are universal. Francis highlights the hope that young people bring to the Church's mission and advocates for an active love that transforms society. His apostolic exhortation is a call to bridge the gap between doctrine and lived experience.

The interdisciplinary work *Catholic Social Teaching and Economic Globalization: The Quest for Alternatives* edited by John Sniegocki critiques economic systems through the lens of Catholic social thought. This collection of essays explores viable alternatives to prevailing economic structures, promoting a vision of justice that aligns with Catholic doctrine's humane ethos.

Finally, for a comprehensive understanding of apologetics in contemporary discourse, Alister McGrath's *Mere Apologetics: How to Help Seekers and Skeptics Find Faith* offers an effective guide. McGrath diagrams the pathways for engaging modern inquiries, rooting apologetic discourse in both classical and emerging theological thought. His work is indispensable for those committed to communicating the faith in an ever-evolving cultural landscape.

This bibliographic journey is an invitation to explore the confluence of ideas shaping the Catholic response to both spiritual and societal questions. Each entry stands as a testament to the ongoing dialogue between tradition and innovation, anchoring faith in the context of everyday challenges and divine aspirations.